International Joint Ve

Copyright ©2014 Klueger and Stein, LLP
All Rights Reserved

ISBN 978-0-9839780-4-6 (paperback)
ISBN 978-0-9839780-5-3 (e-book)

No part of this book may be reproduced in any form or by any electronic or mechanical means, including information shortage and retrieval systems, without permission in writing from the publisher and author. The only exception is by a reviewer, who may quote short excerpts in a review. For permission and rights information, e-mail Mr. Klueger at rklueger@ksilaw.com and Mr. Stein at jstein@ksilaw.com.

Published by Klueger and Stein, LLP
16000 Ventura Boulevard, Suite 1000
Encino, California 91436
United States of America
+1-818-933-3838
www.ksilaw.com

joint venture, and that neither party to the agreement is the agent of the other.

Many joint ventures – and most international joint ventures – are characterized by the creation of a separate entity to act as the joint venture. Thus, Company A and Company B – the joint venturers – will form Company C. Company C will be the JV. As we shall see, considerable thought, and perhaps a great deal of negotiation, will go into determining whether Company C is a separate corporation, a general or limited partnership, a limited liability company, or some combination of these entities.

II.   What is an International Joint Venture ("IJV")?

An IJV can be any joint venture whose partners are resident in different countries, which results in at least one of the partners conducting business in a country other than its home country. However, in this book, an IJV is confined to those joint ventures in which at least one of the partners is a U.S. business and at least one of the other partners is a non-U.S. business, and the business of the joint venture is conducted outside of the U.S., i.e. in the "home" or "local" country of the non-U.S. partner. Many IJV's are conducted in the U.S. and involve foreign partners who desire to enter the U.S. market, but we will not concern ourselves here with those joint ventures. In this book, it is the U.S. partner who will need to concern itself with all of the local customs and local business practices entailed in conducting business abroad. It is the U.S. partner who will have to worry about taxation both in the U.S. and in the "local" country. The "local" partner will concern itself only with its own laws and its own taxes. It will not need to concern itself about U.S. taxation. We will assume that the IJV will <u>not</u> engage in business in the U.S.

Introduction: An Overview of IJVs

I.   What is a Joint Venture?

As a general rule a *joint venture* is the collaborative effort of two or more existing business entities that are united for a long- or short-term economic purpose. Most people have a "gut" sense of what a joint venture is; they know it when they see it. But the term "joint venture" hides more than it reveals. Under U.S. law, a joint venture is a *partnership*, even if the partnership is created for a specific, short-term business purpose. That means that the joint venturers are partners, with the resulting legal consequences. For example, in a partnership, each partner is an *agent* for the partnership, empowered to enter into legal contracts binding the partnership. As we shall see when we discuss the joint venture agreement, if we wish to limit a partner's ability to bind the joint venture (and the other partners) the agreement will need to specify exactly what a partner may and may not do.

Some ventures are of such short duration, and exist for such a limited purpose, that the parties may not consider themselves – and may not be -- partners. For example, a landowner may desire to construct a structure on his property. To do so, he will hire a contractor to build the structure to his specifications. After the structure is completed and the contractor is paid, the landowner and the contractor will go their separate ways. Technically, two businesses have entered into a collaborative effort for a short-term economic purpose. Yet they likely will not think of themselves as having been partners, and certainly will not have considered that they had entered into a joint venture. A lawyer drafting the contract for the landowner should specify that the parties to the contract are not partners, that they have not entered into a partnership or

Table of Contents

III. Why Conduct Business Abroad?

Conducting a business for profit in the U.S. is difficult enough. Why compound the difficulties by conducting business in a foreign country? The answer may seem obvious: By entering into a foreign market, you increase the chances of increased sales. Even if your sales don't increase, lowered manufacturing costs may increase your bottom line. But the answer is more subtle. Entering into foreign markets may be the only way to increase sales if the U.S. market has become saturated. Entering foreign markets may not produce immediate profits, but it will provide you with the opportunity to brand your products globally. Finally, you may have no choice. If you do not sell your products or services globally, your competitors will, placing you at a world-wide competitive disadvantage.

Chapter 1: The Basics of IJV's

I.   Alternatives to IJV's

It is certainly possible to expand sales into a foreign market without entering into an IJV. All that you need to do is sell your products abroad. Finding foreign customers has become easier with the rise of the Internet. Internet payment solutions such as PayPal have proliferated, making payment for the goods shipped easy and relatively certain. All you may need is a freight forwarder to ship the goods, and perhaps not even that.

Obviously, there are limits to the foreign sales that you can generate by such passive means. If you are serious about increasing foreign sales, you will need to be more proactive.

Local Sales Agents

The next step might be to engage a local sales agent. Typically, this agent will be a broker who will generate sales and book orders on a commission; he will not acquire goods for his own account. He may, but very often will not, warehouse your and other sellers' products. He may, but very often will not, work on an exclusive basis. How much time, effort and expense he puts into generating sales will be up to him. He may provide prospective customers with your sales catalog, or he may invest in generating a catalog of his own.

Right from the beginning there is a serious tax issue that arises when a U.S. manufacturer engages a local sales agent: Does engaging a local sales agent constitute "doing business" in the local market, subjecting the U.S. seller to local *income taxes*? We can assume that local sales are subject to local sales and VAT taxes; having the U.S. seller subject to local income taxes on the local sales may be unacceptable.

The U.S. has entered into income tax treaties with most of the world's countries that are not tax havens. Income tax treaties exist for one principal purpose: to assure that two countries do not attempt to tax the same income. Most income tax treaties contain the concept of the *permanent establishment.* If a foreign entity maintains "permanent establishment" in the local market, the foreign entity will be subject to local income taxes on its local sales. Under most income tax treaties, engaging a local sales agent will not constitute a permanent establishment, and will not result in the foreign seller being subject to local income taxes. Nevertheless, there are some "do's and don'ts" that foreign sellers should follow when engaging a local sales agent, as follows:

• *The local sales agent should not have the authority to approve a sale.* All sales contracts should specify that all that the local agent is doing is soliciting orders, with final approval of every contract being with the agent's principal in the U.S. It may seem formulaic, (and it is) but technically it's the difference between entering into contracts in the local country or entering into contracts in the U.S.

• *The local agent should be an independent agent.* If the local agent engages in no business other than your business, it appears that you are engaging in local business through your controlled agent. This is especially true if the local agent has an office, and the office displays your business logo and your business name and is listed in the local telephone directory. In fact, a controlled agent with a local office might indicate that you do have a permanent establishment in the local market, subjecting you to local income tax.

• *Set up a separate local entity to provide local services.* There are many instances in which selling products into the local market is not sufficient. You may be required to install, service and repair the items sold. If that is the case, consider forming a separate entity for the purpose of providing these services. The separate entity would contract with you to provide the services to your customers. The separate entity would pay taxes in the local country on the income it receives. However, you will have minimized the risk that you are deemed to have established a permanent establishment in the local market.

Not all income tax treaties are the same. For example, Denmark may have an income tax treaty with Norway that is more favorable than Norway's income tax treaty with the U.S. A U.S. seller may wish to conduct business in Norway. Some U.S. sellers engage in *treaty shopping* by establishing a foreign subsidiary in the country with the favorable treaty. In this example, the U.S. seller would establish a subsidiary in Denmark solely to avail itself of the favorable Denmark-Norway tax treaty. The Internal Revenue Service frowns upon treaty shopping and is very aggressive in trying to stamp it out. The U.S. will not grant a seller the benefits of a tax treaty if the IRS determines that one of the treaty partners has no real business connection to the treaty country.

Licensing to Local Distributors or Manufacturers

Simply engaging a local sales agent may not be sufficient to generate sales in the local market. The next step up may be licensing your trademark, formula, designs, etc. to a local manufacturer or distributor, permitting the local manufacturer to sell your products under your brand. In exchange for the grant of the license, you will receive a *royalty* for every product sold.

The extent to which the local country will have the right to tax the royalty (and require the local payor to withhold the required tax before remitting it abroad) is likely governed by the income tax treaty between the U.S. and the local country. The tax treaty may eliminate or reduce the tax on the royalty. For example, under the income tax treaty between China and the U.S., China may impose a 10% tax on royalties generated from licensing in China. Under the U.S.-Netherlands treaty, no tax on royalties may be imposed, provided that you do not have a permanent establishment in the other country, as it is defined in the treat. And under the U.S.-India tax treaty, India may impose taxes on royalties ranging from 10% to 20%, depending on the source of the royalties. Needless to say, no one should enter into business in a foreign country without knowing exactly how the tax treaty purports to tax profits in that country. This is a refrain that will be repeated often in this book.

If all that you do is license your brands in return for a royalty, you probably have not entered into an IJV, and if that is the case, the licensing and royalty agreement should specify that the parties have not entered into a joint venture and are not each others' partners or agents. But the distance between a contract for the licensing of brands and an actual IJV is often not very great. If both parties are required to commit capital, or if mutual management is designated in the license agreement, the "licensing agreement" may in fact be an IJV.

II.   Advantages and Disadvantages of IJV's vs. Local Subsidiaries

The principal advantage of hiring a local sales agent or licensing intellectual property or technology to a local manufacturer or distributor is that the commitment of capital, time and effort are kept to a minimum. If the effort proves unsuccessful, you can most likely pull the plug without having committed too much. A second advantage is that by not actually engaging in business in the local market, you are not subject to income taxation in that market. At worst, your local sales will be subject to local sales taxes and, in the case of a royalty arrangement, the royalties you receive may be subject to local tax and withholding. [As we shall see later, you may be able to offset the local taxes by means of the *foreign tax credit*].

Selling through a local agent or entering into a royalty arrangement represents one extreme on the continuum of commitment. At the other end of the continuum is the wholly-owned corporate subsidiary established in the local market. If "American Brands" establishes "American Brands – Mexico" as a wholly-owned subsidiary to conduct business in Mexico, there is no question that Mexico will be entitled to tax all of American Brands – Mexico's profits as fully as if it were owned by Mexican citizens. American Brands can establish a Mexican subsidiary by creating it. Alternatively, it can acquire a local business that already conducts the business that American Brands intends to conduct, either by outright acquisition or by merging with the existing entity. In either event, American Brands' commitment is total. If the local subsidiary is profitable, all of the profits inure to American Brands. If the local subsidiary is a failure, American Brands shares the cost of failure with no one. But just as it shares the costs of success or failure with no one, it shares control with no one. It alone makes all of the management decisions; it does not need to defer to the wishes or sensibilities of a local partner.

Midway between the lowest level of commitment, i.e. selling through a local agent or distributor, and the highest level of commitment, i.e. establishing or acquiring a local subsidiary, is the IJV. If American Brands finds a local partner, and American Brands and the local partner are equal owners of "AM – Mexico," it is likely that American Brands' commitment of capital, time and energy will be less than if it establishes or acquires a local subsidiary. Of course, if American Brands and its local partners are equal partners, American Brands will be entitled to receive 50%, not 100%, of the profits generated by the joint venture. But American Brands will likely not be able to make all of the management decisions. Its local partner will want – and should have – considerable discretion in the day-to-day operations of the IJV.

One of the biggest perceived advantages of the wholly-owned subsidiary over the IJV is the ability to control one's technology and intellectual property. Many U.S. firms believe that they simply cannot run the risk of sharing their technology with a local partner. There is a widely-held belief that local partners cannot be trusted to safeguard technology entrusted to them and that their local partners might use the shared technology to become competitors, to the point of even using the acquired technology to compete not only in the local market, but in third markets, including the U.S. itself. For this reason, many U.S. businesses, particularly those who can afford to shoulder all of the costs of establishing or acquiring a local subsidiary, prefer to do so rather than forming an IJV with a local partner.

It is possible, of course, to form an IJV and still protect your technology, trade secrets and other intellectual property. For one, the joint venture agreement can provide that the local partner will not compete with the U.S. partner in the local market or in any other market. If that is not sufficient, it may be possible for you to simply not share the technology with the local partner, and instead *license* the technology and trade secrets to the local partner, either for a nominal royalty or for an actual royalty.

III. Are the JV Partners Ever Equal?

It is rarely the case that both parties to a joint venture have equal clout. Far more often, one party to the IJV is larger, is better capitalized and is more experienced than its prospective partner. It is likely that one party "needs" the deal more than the other. For example, a U.S. manufacturer may find that if it wishes to enter into a local market, it must team up with a local distributor uniquely situated to distribute its products, and if it cannot team up with that distributor, it cannot enter the local market. The local distributor may have scores of other customers, and the revenue produced by the U.S. manufacturer may represent only a small increase in its sales. Of course, the reverse is often true. A U.S. manufacturer may be able to select among scores of local distributors.

It is often the case that it is only in the negotiations leading to the formation of the IJV that the parties learn who "needs" the deal more, and who has the bigger clout. But whether negotiating from relative strength or relative weakness, negotiating an IJV is very different than negotiating a merger or an acquisition. Most American lawyers, when assisting in the purchase or sale of a business, will instinctively try to get the "best" deal for their clients. An experienced lawyer will assure himself and his client that every possible risk has been eliminated or ameliorated. That's what lawyers do. But it is possible to negotiate an IJV *too well*! Lawyers and their clients should remember the fundamental difference between mergers and acquisitions versus IJV's. In most cases, when the negotiations for a purchase or sale are concluded, the relationship with the other party is concluded. When the negotiations leading to the formation of an IJV are concluded, the relationship is only beginning. If the negotiations are successful, each side must feel satisfied by the result. If a partner feels abused, it is not likely that the partner will commit totally to the relationship. Remember: *Fifty percent of all joint ventures fail*! The ones that have a better chance of success are the ones where the dominant party did not try to squeeze every possible advantage out of the negotiations, but instead assured itself that its partner was happy and committed to the relationship.

When negotiating an IJV, American lawyers need to refocus their definitions of success. Not only must the relationship work for both partners, it must also work in more than one country. If the structure is tax-efficient in the U.S. for the American partner, but is a tax disaster for the foreign partner, the foreign partner will soon lose interest in the deal. IJV's are collaborative, not competitive efforts. That means that the lawyers must modify their usual instincts and practices.

IV.   Finding the JV Partner

In a majority of cases, the parties to an IJV have had a pre-existing relationship before they form an IJV. Typically, one may have been the supplier to the other, or one may have been the customer of the other, and they now wish to make their relationship more formal and perhaps more exclusive. Indeed, they may have initially viewed their customer/supplier relationship as a trial period leading to an IJV. In many cases, however, the IJV's have had no prior business relationship, but have instead been introduced by an investment banker, attorney or accountant.

When parties have had a relationship prior to entering into the IJV, the fact that they have had a relationship can be something of a trap. The parties may feel that they "know" each other, resulting in the parties ignoring the rigorous due diligence that the parties must conduct before they finalize the agreement. That rigorous due diligence is outlined in the following chapter.

Chapter 2: International Due Diligence

I.   Introduction

As any attorney or investment banker will tell you, there is *nothing* more important than due diligence. Time and time again purchasers and sellers (especially purchasers) of businesses overlook or ignore one fact that results in the difference between profit and no profit or overlook one item that would have steered them away from the deal or at least would have altered the price they were willing to pay. Very often the one undiscovered and/or undisclosed fact leads to litigation.

As critical and as difficult as due diligence is, it is at least twice as difficult when the object of the due diligence is an IJV. If the prospective partner is based in the U.S., all that you need to do is perform due diligence on the prospective partner. You don't need to perform due diligence on your prospective partner's *country*; presumably, you know all about that country. But if you contemplate selling in a foreign ("local") market you certainly do not know as much about the local market as you do about the U.S. market, and you undoubtedly do not know as much about the local market as your prospective partner.

So your due diligence needs to focus both on your prospective partner and on the local market itself. Here's a tip: Don't allow your attorneys, investment bankers and other professionals to conduct their due diligence from a boilerplate due diligence checklist. At best, it's a waste of time, and at worst it is insulting to your prospective partner. If your partner has three employees and $200,000 in annual sales, you look foolish asking your partner if it has ever been investigated by local anti-trust authorities. Tailor your due diligence to the proposed business relationship, not to a canned checklist.

II. Local Market Due Diligence – A Case Study

We have all heard horror stories about foreign sellers who flopped in a foreign country. There are as many reasons for the failure as there are horror stories. All of these horror stories have one thing in common: the lack of due diligence.

In the late1970's, we represented a major manufacturer of disposable diapers. It sold diapers throughout the U.S. At that time, our client learned that not a single disposable diaper was available for sale in the country of Venezuela. Mothers of infants used diaper services or washed cloth diapers themselves. Our client conducted intensive market research in Venezuela, and concluded that there was no cultural impediment to selling disposable diapers there. Mothers both in Caracas and in small villages were as eager to accept a solution to re-usable cloth diapers as were American mothers in the 1950's and 1960's, when disposable diapers completely displaced cloth diapers in very short order.

Our client began offering its disposable diapers in Venezuela – and nothing happened. Despite extensive marketing and educational efforts, (and absolutely no competition) our client's disposable diapers seemed to be nailed to the shelves.

Then our client received a telephone call from one of its local sales agents in charge of selling some of my client's other products in Venezuela. Of course, he had not been consulted throughout the due diligence process, because he was in charge of other products. But he had seen the diapers on the shelves, and immediately saw the problem. There was nothing wrong with the diapers. The problem lay in the packaging (the "put-up"). There was no problem; he informed us, in selling packages of 18 or 36 diapers in the U.S. But Venezuela was a poor country. Would it be possible, the agent asked, for my client to offer diapers in packages of 3 or 6? Our client did a quick "back-of-the-envelope" calculation of the number of babies born in Venezuela every year, and immediately concluded there would be no problem in modifying the packaging for Venezuela. Packages of 3 and 6 diapers began flying off the shelves.

This case study teaches two lessons. First, you cannot conduct too much due diligence. There is always something that you are going to miss. Your hope is that what you miss is correctable and isn't fatal to the venture. More importantly, it teaches that there is no substitute for having local people in positions of authority assisting in your local business, regardless of the manner in which the business is conducted. If you build your own local manufacturing plant or create your own distribution network from scratch, it is critical to have knowledgeable local people on the ground in positions of authority. The alternative is forever trying to sell packages of 36 disposable diapers in Venezuela and forever wondering why they won't sell.

III.   Your Due Diligence Team

Your due diligence should have three components: "operational," "financial" and "legal." Due diligence isn't complete until all three have been conducted. The key is to have the right people perform the right tasks. The operational due diligence should be performed by the people who are going to be on the ground in the local market on a day-to-day basis. They need to familiarize themselves with the customer and supplier relationships, the manufacturing and sales force, and the myriad other factors necessary to bring the IJV's goods or services to market. It sounds obvious, but too often the due diligence is conducted solely by a senior executive (or the owner) who will have little oversight of the actual operations of the business.

The financial due diligence should be performed by your controller and/or outside auditors. Herein lies a trap: American auditors are comfortable with American accounting and auditing standards, and they often assume that auditing standards are uniform. They are not. What may appear to be "audited" financial statements may be something that would not qualify as such in the U.S. It is imperative that your auditors first determine what are the local accounting standards before they begin to examine your partner's books.

The legal due diligence should be performed by your legal counsel, who should interface with the partner's counsel. In most cases, your counsel should engage outside counsel and accountants who are knowledgeable with respect to local tax, regulatory and foreign exchange issues. The one thing you should not ask of your counsel (we are asked this all the time) is whether he or she believes that the price is right. Lawyers are not investment bankers, and most do not have the skills to make an informed judgment as to whether the deal makes financial sense.

The one thing that every transactional attorney hates is to be brought into the deal too late. I once called a seller's attorney to advise him that I had some difficulties with some of the representations in a proposed definitive agreement and wished to revise them, only to be informed that the "proposed" definitive agreement had actually been signed, and that my role was to assist in the closing. Very embarrassing.

It may sound obvious, but the members of your operational, financial and legal due diligence team should coordinate with each other, and often they do not. We hate to do it, especially in writing, but here we are going to fess up to a due diligence failure that we participated in, which resulted from the failure of the members of our client's due diligence team to coordinate with each other. Some years ago, one of our clients acquired a company that manufactured tea. As part of our legal and operational due diligence, we required the seller to disclose to us in writing every ingredient that went into every variety of the seller's teas. This the seller did. What turned out not to be exactly true (it turned out to be mostly false) were the *percentages* of the different ingredients in each variety of tea, a fact that was not revealed until our client began testing the various brands *after the closing*. The result of the incorrect disclosure was that the cost of producing the various brands would be far greater than my client had anticipated. What made all of this worse is that had our auditors compared the seller's purchase invoices with the disclosures that the seller made to the lawyers, it would have been obvious to us that the disclosure of the percentages of the different ingredients could not possibly have been accurate. Had the lawyers worked more closely with the auditors, the false disclosure could have been discovered prior to closing. We could have avoided the litigation that ensued.

IV.   Local Market Due Diligence – A Checklist

Whatever are the costs in terms of hard dollars, time and energy that are expended in the pursuit of a domestic joint venture; these are compounded exponentially in the pursuit of an IJV. U.S. firms who have sold products or services into a local market – often for years or decades – may delude themselves into believing that they know the local market well enough to form an IJV with a local partner without conducting a thorough due diligence review of the local market itself. The costs of failure are far greater than the due diligence costs. No one ever saved money cutting corners on due diligence. Here is a checklist of local market considerations.

• *Are there restrictions on foreign direct investment*? The very first thing that anyone contemplating an IJV needs to consider is whether the local government will permit the investment at all. The "government" can be either the national government or a state or regional government that has the effective power to block foreign direct investment ("FDI").

Restrictions on FDI can take many forms. The most basic is an outright prohibition on foreign ownership. If you are thinking of investing in the petroleum sector in Mexico or in fishing in Iceland, think again. Many countries (including the U.S.) have prohibitions on foreign investment in sectors considered sensitive from a national security standpoint, such as aviation and telecommunications. Sometimes, the prohibitions on FDI do not seem to have any rational basis. Brazil permits foreign ownership of real estate, but not of real estate that is located within 150 kilometers of a national border.

It is easy enough to deal with restrictions on FDI that are explicit, i.e., in writing. It is much more difficult to determine which local approval, permitting or screening processes constitute effective prohibitions on FDI. For example, Japan requires potential foreign investors in certain industries to provide proof that their FDI will be an economic benefit to the country. Mexico requires similar pre-clearance for the foreign acquisition of a majority stake in a local business. Some local pre-clearance requirements are not rigorously enforced; others are. Potential investors ignore these requirements at their peril. As we shall see later, the U.S. Foreign Corrupt Practices Act makes skirting these local restrictions risky and expensive.

Even if the local country does not place a formal prohibition on FDI, it can effectively prohibit FDI if it controls the involvement of foreign nationals in the local business. If your managers will have difficulty entering the country, the fact that the IJV is legal will do you no good. Similarly, even if they can enter the country, if there are restrictions on their employment – such as the employment of foreign nationals in Turkey -- the fact that your people can enter the country may be a meaningless benefit. Even if your managers and employees can enter the country and work there, you may not be permitted to control the entity. For example, in the countries comprising the European Union, local residents must form a majority of the boards of directors of insurance companies.[1]

Formal restrictions on FDI are diminishing, especially in the manufacturing sector but they are still robust in many countries in the service sector.

---

[1] These requirements often produce absurd results. In order to comply with an EU requirement that a director have an actual residence address (and not merely a postal box) within the EU, we were once required to lease an apartment within the EU in the director's name. For all the years that he was a director, the monthly rent was timely paid for a tenant who never once set foot in his residence (or in the country, for that matter.) The leasing agent no doubt wondered who this mystery man was and why he never used his apartment.

Some countries, while not imposing formal or informal restrictions on FDI investment, do impose *minimum* capital requirements, ranging from a few thousand dollars in South Korea to hundreds of thousands in some of the ASEAN countries.

• *Are there currency restrictions or restrictions on the repatriation of profits?* The U.S. has never imposed any restrictions on any person, be it a U.S. citizen or a foreigner, from removing dollars from the U.S.[2] Consequently, currency controls are something with which many U.S. business persons have no experience. It is one thing to be able to conduct business in a foreign country. It is quite another thing to be able to remove your profits from the foreign country. Needless to say, most U.S. business owners would prefer to receive their profits in U.S. dollars.

Brazil is typical of the currency restrictions that many countries place on the repatriation of profits. Within 30 days of the foreign investment in an IJV, the foreign investment must be registered with the Central Bank. If the foreign partner is a U.S. corporation or individual, the registration must be made in U.S. dollars. The foreign investment is given a control number, which is used to track the inflow and outflow of currency. If foreign investment is made in Brazil without the required registration, there is no way that the profits may be lawfully removed from Brazil, a fact that provides a strong motivation to comply with the law. If the initial FDI has been duly registered, there is no restriction on the removal of the profits, with one notable exception. If the value of

---

[2] The Bank Secrecy Act does, however, impose reporting requirements on the removal of currency.

the currency being removed is equal or less than the initial investment, there is no restriction on repatriation. But if the value of the currency removed exceeds the value of the currency registered, it is considered profit and taxed at a 15% rate.

Many countries impose restrictions on the ability of local businesses to convert local currency into U.S. dollars. Many also prohibit local residents to possess more than a small amount of U.S. dollars. These restrictions may result in a difficulty in paying local managers – who may be your employees assigned to the IJV – in U.S. dollars. If the local currency is not convertible into U.S. dollars, your on-site employees may hold what is essentially worthless paper when their local employment ends. All of these matters must be considered before you send employees into a local market, not after.

• *How onerous are local employment laws*? Many U.S. business owners complain about federal and state employment laws. They are inconsequential compared to the requirements and restrictions that are placed upon many foreign businesses relative to the compensation, benefits, working conditions and worker rights granted to employees in these countries. These range from requirements for paid vacations, paid holidays, paid training, paid sick pay, and paid maternity leave, to job protection rights requiring government approval in order to terminate an employee to long advance notice requirements before a business can be relocated or moved. What is worse, IJV's conducting business in any of the countries of the EU might find themselves dealing with a representative of the employees, a "works council," something that resembles a labor union but which isn't one, and which is foreign to any U.S. business. Each of the EU countries is authorized to enact its own works council legislation, but at the very least a business confronted with a works council will be required to consult with it before making many business decisions, and at its worst will give the works council the right to veto many decisions that U.S. business owners assume is the sole province of management.

The rights that employees do or do not have within a particular jurisdiction may determine whether it is the IJV or the local partner who actually employs and compensates the employees. If you believe that there are real employment liabilities lurking in the country in the local market, it is best, if possible, to structure the transaction so that your IJV partner – and not the IJV itself – is the employer, and it is your IJV partner who compensates the employees, deals with the works council, establishes the working conditions, etc.

• *Are local anti-trust laws an impediment?* Many countries regulate mergers and acquisitions to the same extent as their U.S. counterpart, The Hart-Scott-Rodino Antitrust Improvements Act of 1976. Within the EU, the *EU Merger Control Regulation* applies to "concentrations" that "threaten to affect significantly competition in a market of a Member State." IJV's are explicitly included within the purview of the Merger Control Regulation. As with Hart-Scott-Rodino, consultations with local authorities are encouraged before a commitment of funds and effort is made.

• *Is there a local "special economic zone"?* Some countries provide one or more special economic zones within the country, either an entire city or part of a city.[3]

------

[3] China has made the entire province of Hainan Island a special economic zone.

These special economic zones exist for one reason: to lure foreign direct investment. Within such a zone, it is usual that tax incentives exist, exchange controls are relaxed and/or limitations on foreign investment are abrogated.

V. Prospective Partner Due Diligence – A Checklist

Every bit as important as the due diligence of the country in which the IJV will conduct business is the due diligence on your prospective partner itself. Very often, a successful pre-existing supplier, distributor or customer relationship has existed, which may lead you to believe that you "know" your prospective partner. This should not take the place of extensive due diligence on your partner. The contemplated relationship will be very different from the prior relationship. Here is a checklist.

• *Is your prospective partner trustworthy?* If you cannot trust your partner, nothing else matters. You cannot learn whether your potential partner will steal your intellectual property from your potential partner. If your prospective partner has already burned through one or more foreign partners, you would like to know that. That's why it is imperative to engage knowledgeable local legal counsel and auditors right from the start.

• *Is your prospective partner's corporate culture compatible with yours?* Every business has a corporate culture. Some businesses know what their corporate culture is, and often tout it as an asset virtue. In some businesses, the employees know full well what the corporate culture is, even if management does not. A prospective partner's corporate culture may work for it, but it may not be a corporate culture you are comfortable working with. In any event, job one must be to determine the prospective partner's corporate culture. This cannot be done from a distance, and cannot be accomplished in a lawyer's office. Your key managers who will be interfacing with their local counterparts on a day-in-day basis must visit the local business and should spend many days (preferably weeks) seeing how the local business is operated. They must obtain an understanding of how management deals with employees (and labor unions and works councils, if any). They must determine if the production standards are compatible with yours. Needless to say, they must determine if there are any unusual or illegal business practices with which local management is comfortable with but which you are not. You cannot learn this working off of a due diligence checklist; you need to be there.

• *Is your prospective partner's access to raw materials, parts and suppliers adequate to handle the increased business*? If your prospective partner is a local manufacturer, it is likely that the proposed IJV contemplates what may be a substantial increase in its output. If the proposed partner does not have the ability to access the raw materials, parts and supplies necessary to achieve the higher level of output, the venture will fail, even if your local partner benefits from the increased volume. Similarly, it is pointless to ramp up production if the local partner's ability to deliver the increased production to market is exceeded.

Just as it is inherently risky for any U.S. manufacturer to rely on a sole source of parts or raw materials, the IJV could fail if your local partner relies upon a sole source of supply, especially if that sole source determines that it doesn't wish to sell to a foreigner.

Your local partner may sell its products or services through a local sales force. That sales force may be adequate for its current level of sales, but may be wholly inadequate for the increased level of sales that the IJV contemplates. If an increase in the sales force is necessary, is such an increase feasible? And if so, how long will it take to ramp up the sales force, and what will it cost?

• *Is your prospective partner reliant upon one or two key managers?* As we all know, not every business owner actually runs the business. Very often, the fact that it is difficult to pull the owner off the golf course is not a detriment to the smooth operation of the business; his absence may enhance it. But if your prospective partner is run by one or two key managers, that is a fact that you must ascertain before you commit to the IJV. If the local partner is in fact run by a key employee, you must determine if that employee will continue with the IJV after it is formed.

Even if the business is not run by one or two key managers, it is often a mistake to rely solely upon the owner or chief executive of the business in the conduct of your operational due diligence. You should always get the perspective of the people on the factory floor and in the sales offices.

• *Can the current plant accommodate increased production?* That's obvious. Here is what is not so obvious: If the plant is leased, when will the lease expire? If the lease will expire shortly, can the lease be renewed on favorable terms? If there is doubt as to whether a lease can be renewed, are there alternative premises to which to relocate if need be?

• *Is your prospective partner compliant in all employment, tax and regulatory matters?* U.S. businesses often enter into IJV's assuming that if their partner has a problem with local tax collectors or other regulators, it's their partner's problem, not theirs. That's a very short-sighted approach. For starters, your local partner may avoid the payment of its proper tax liability by making unauthorized payments to tax collectors that you might not be willing to make (you may not be prepared to violate the Foreign Corrupt Practices Act). The fact that your local partner may have successfully underpaid its taxes in the past is no guarantee that it will be able to so in the future. Even if you cannot be held directly liable for your partner's prior tax liability, there is no guarantee that a local tax collector may not be able to seize IJV property or shut down your partner for non-payment of taxes.

Many U.S. businesspersons are reticent to probe their prospective partner's past practices. Often, the local partner evidences dismay at the apparent lack of trust that the Americans have for their putative partners, especially in countries where mutual trust is more important than written agreements. If we represent a client who does not wish to appear rude and/or mistrustful of its putative partner, we advise our client to "make us the bad guy." That is, we advise my client to inform his partner that while he trusts his counterpart, his lawyer insists on doing his job and will not allow his client to close the deal until he is satisfied that all of the taxes have been paid, all of the permits that are required to conduct the business have been obtained, etc. By the time the deal closes, my client's partner make not care much for us, but that is a small price to pay for proper due diligence.

In some countries – including all of the developed ones -- you can verify whether a government audit is underway and/or whether all of the taxes that are owed have been paid. In some countries, it's not that easy. Needless to say, you or your due diligence team need to determine that all of the taxes have been paid and all of the licenses and permits necessary to operate the business have been obtained before you make a substantial investment in a foreign country.

• *How financially strong is your partner?* Entrepreneurs are optimists by nature. But it doesn't hurt prior to finalizing an IJV to ask whether your local partner is financially strong enough to survive a downturn, or whether you will have to bail out your partner if there is a downturn. If possible, you should obtain your partner's five most recent years' financial statements prior to finalizing the deal. As indicated previously, if the financial statements purport to be "audited," the people on your financial due diligence team need to ascertain that the auditing standards in the local country are comparable to the U.S. auditing standards.

• *Is your partner ahead or behind the tech curve?* This is especially true if the IJV is being formed for the principal purpose of exploiting technology and bringing an as-yet undeveloped product to market.

• *Are all of the partner's intellectual property and technology protected by patents, trademarks, etc?* Determining that all of the IP that each partner owns and/or the IJV will develop is protected by patents, trademarks, copyrights, etc. is a key function of the legal due diligence team. The IP due diligence consists of a number a separate inquiries, among which are:

•• Does your partner actually own the critical IP rights? It is possible that the rights to a patent are owned by an employee, who never actually assigned the patent to his employer. It's embarrassing to learn this after the IJV has been formed.

•• Has your partner licensed the rights to someone else? What's worse, has the partner licensed the rights to a competitor? Even if your partner owns the local rights to a patent or trademark, he may not own the rights in a third country into which you might wish to expand the IJV.

•• Are any of the IP rights subject to infringement claims? Conversely, your partner may believe that some other party is infringing on its IP. If your partner is contemplating litigation, you should know of it.

•• When, if at all, do the rights to critical IP expire under local law? It is possible that the rights to a patent or trademark may be preserved in perpetuity by maintaining a minimum level of sales and by making a payment. But if the use of IP may sunset for whatever reason, you need to know that before you finalize an IJV to use that IP.

Most lawyers have their favorite war stories about deals that soured because of IP due diligence that wasn't properly performed, or wasn't performed at all. Here's ours. In 1998, Volkswagen acquired the *assets* of Rolls Royce and Bentley. They paid $800 million for most of the hard assets necessary to manufacture these brands. But after the deal closed, Volkswagen learned – to its horror – that the $800 million price tag did not include the rights to the "Rolls Royce" trademarks, which meant that Volkswagen could build a car that looked exactly like a Rolls Royce; they just couldn't call it one!

Here's another. In 1990 Clorox Corporation acquired the business and trademarks of Pine-Sol. Clorox purchased Pine-Sol in the hopes of expanding the Pine-Sol brand into new areas. Only after the deal closed did Clorox learn of a 30-year old agreement that Pine-Sol had entered into with another party that restricted the use of the Pine-Sol brand to disinfectants. As a result, Clorox could use the Pine-Sol brand, but not for the exact purpose for which Clorox had made the acquisition.

• *How politically connected is your partner?* We owe this bit of wisdom to one of the most successful transactional attorneys in India. He advises that when contemplating an IJV in India, you need to know if your potential partner is "in" with the local political party, which is going to make life easy, or on the "outs," which is going to make life difficult. You need to learn this from outside local counsel, not from your partner. The worst that can happen is that your local partner was part of the "in" crowd, but that as a result of shifting local political fortunes, your partner is now on the outside looking in, and may need the IJV with you to survive.

Conclusion

In all honesty, it never dawned on us how important it is to be politically connected at the local level in India until our Indian attorney friend told us so. The point is that you cannot know everything, and you will never know as much about a foreign country as you do your own. You may have thought that you had asked everything, only to learn that there is something obvious to everyone in the local market that is not obvious to you. That's why it is imperative to engage local attorneys and accountants to assist you with respect to every aspect of the search, planning, negotiations, structuring and operations of an IJV. You must rely on your own local people, not on the local people who work for your IJV partner.

Chapter 3: Structuring the International Joint Venture

I.   Introduction

Let's assume that you have found your local partner and have completed all the due diligence you feel you need to do. The next step is to determine the form of the IJV.

We saw in Chapter 1 that it is possible – and commonplace – to conduct business in a local market without the necessity of a formal joint venture. A U.S. business can license its technology and/or intellectual property to a local manufacturer or distributor and receive a royalty in return. The royalty payments are, of course, subject to immediate U.S. taxation, because U.S. taxpayers (individual U.S. citizens and resident aliens, U.S.-chartered corporations and U.S. partnerships and limited liability companies) are subject to immediate taxation on their world-wide earnings. It is also possible that the country in which the royalties were earned might withhold a portion of the royalty payments for local taxes, a result that might be overcome by a tax treaty between the U.S. and the local country.

The advantage of a licensing arrangement is that it minimizes the U.S. licensor's risk and expense. The disadvantage is that it also minimizes the opportunity for profit, limiting the revenues to the royalties. The tax disadvantage is that there is no opportunity to *defer* the incidence of U.S. taxation. You are taxed on the royalties when you receive them.

A U.S. manufacturer desiring a more active presence in the local market might engage a local agent to assist it in generating sales. As we have already seen, the tax risk in engaging a local agent might result in the U.S.

manufacturer being deemed to have a *permanent establishment* in the local market, resulting in all of the U.S. manufacturer's profits being taxed in the local market. It is probable that the U.S. manufacturer will qualify for the *foreign tax credit*, thus offsetting the tax imposed in the local country. But there is still no possibility of deferral.

From a tax standpoint, a U.S. business seeking to structure an IJV has three *tax* goals, apart from all of its operational goals:

- *Minimize foreign taxes* i.e. the taxes imposed in the local market;
- *Defer U.S. taxes;* and
- *Maximize foreign tax credits*

When a U.S. business is negotiating an IJV with a local partner, the partners' operational goals are usually congruent: they each wish to maximize sales and profits with a minimum of legal exposure. But the tax goals of the U.S. partner and its local partner may be divergent, resulting in some hard bargaining over the structure of the IJV.

II.   A (Mercifully Brief) Overview of "Controlled Foreign Corporations" ("CFC's")

The U.S. taxes its individual citizens and resident aliens, as well as domestic corporations, partnerships and LLC's, on their world-wide income. Here are some examples that prove the point:

Example #1: Mr. Garcia, a citizen of Brazil, holds a U.S. "green card." In 2012, he resided full time in Brazil, and all of his income in 2012 resulted from earnings and salary derived from Brazil.

Mr. Garcia is liable for U.S. taxation on all of his 2012 earnings.

Example #2: XYZ, Inc. is a California corporation. In 2012, it owned and operated a hotel in Mexico. It conducted no other business.

XYZ, Inc. is liable for U.S. tax on all of the profits from the operation of its Mexico hotel.

The U.S. has the right to tax its individual citizens and resident aliens and businesses chartered in the U.S. It does not, however, have the right to tax corporations chartered outside of the U.S., unless that corporation is engaged in a trade or business in the U.S., in which case the U.S. can tax only earnings from U.S. sources.

Example #3: Cinco, S.A. is a Mexico corporation. It operates a hotel in Mexico and a hotel in Baltimore. The U.S. can tax Cinco's profits from its Baltimore hotel, but not from its Mexico hotel.

The interplay of these rules led many U.S. taxpayers to ponder setting up foreign corporations in which to conduct their foreign operations. This made especial good sense if the country in which the foreign corporation was chartered was itself a *tax haven* i.e. did not impose its own taxes at all. It is this exact scenario that resulted in the enactment of Subpart F of the Internal Revenue Code. The centerpiece of Subpart F is the "controlled foreign corporation," ("CFC") a concept that exists only in Subpart F.

A CFC is a corporation chartered outside of the U.S. in which more than 50% of the shareholders are "United States persons," i.e. U.S. citizens, resident aliens, corporations chartered by one of the 50 states, and domestic partnerships. But here's where it starts to get complicated. For the purposes of the CFC, you are counted as a "United States shareholder" only if you are a United States person who owns 10% or more of the stock of the foreign corporation. If there are not enough "United States shareholders" holding 10% or more of the stock to equal greater than 50% of all of the stock of the corporation, the corporation cannot be a CFC. Here are some examples that illustrate the rule:

Example #4: XYZ, an Italian Societa per Azioni, is owned by 11 U.S. citizens, each of whom owns 9.9% of the stock.
Because none of them owns 10% of the stock, XYZ has no "U.S. shareholders," and XYZ is not a CFC.

Example #5: ABC, a Denmark Aktieselskab, is owned 50% by XYZ, a California corporation, and 50% by a Danish corporation.
Because XYZ owns only 50%, and not more than 50% of ABC, ABC is not a CFC.

As you can see from this example, the percentage of ownership of an IJV can be critical from a tax standpoint. As we shall see shortly, had XYZ owned more than 50% rather than 50% of ABC, ABC would have been a CFC, and the tax effects on XYZ's shareholders might change dramatically, all for the worse.

Example #6: DEF, a Jamaica Public Limited Company, is a wholly-owned subsidiary of XY\Z, a California corporation.
DEF is a CFC.

This example highlights the obvious, <u>viz</u>, that every foreign subsidiary of a U.S. corporation is a CFC.

What is the result of a foreign corporation being a CFC? If the foreign corporation is a CFC, the U.S. still has no jurisdiction to tax the foreign earnings of the CFC. But the U.S. may subject the U.S. shareholders to their *pro rata* share of the CFC's annual earnings, *even if those earnings are not distributed to the U.S. shareholders*! The hypothetical distributions are often referred to as "constructive dividends," but they're not. They're worse than dividends, which are taxed at lower rates than "ordinary" income. The deemed distributions from a CFC are taxed at the higher ordinary income rates.

That's the bad news. The good news is that not all income earned by a CFC is subject to constructive dividend treatment. The U.S. shareholders of a CFC are subject to taxation only on the CFC's "Subpart F" income.

III.   Subpart F Income

The rationale behind Subpart F of the Internal Revenue Code is the notion that if anyone wished to artificially avoid the payment of U.S. income tax, he or she would do so by incorporating a business in a tax haven and making believe that the business is actually operated from the tax haven. To take an egregious example, if Big Steel, Inc., which operates a plant in Pittsburgh, were to incorporate "BS Caymans" in the Cayman Islands, which imposes no tax, BS Caymans would have to make believe that it is actually manufacturing steel in the Cayman Islands. The assumption is that Big Steel, Inc. would never seek to avoid its U.S. taxes by incorporating in a foreign country that actually imposes its own taxes. The further assumption is that in order to make believe that it is actually operating in the tax haven, BS Caymans would need to engage in certain non-arm's length transactions with either the suppliers of steel or the purchasers of the manufactured steel, for the obvious reason that it is not possible to actually manufacture steel in the Cayman Islands. BS Caymans would most likely have to "purchase" steel from its parent, Big Steel. It might also avoid U.S. taxes by selling steel to a Big Steel affiliate in a foreign country, trapping the earnings in the Cayman Islands, which imposes no tax on the earnings. The diagram on the following page illustrates the classic Subpart F income arrangement.

Here's the bottom line: Subpart F income is comprised of earnings by a CFC in a country other than the country in which it is chartered, from transactions involving a related party, in a no-tax or low-tax jurisdiction. Subpart F income includes *"foreign base company sales income,"* and *"foreign base company service income,"* but the two are essentially the same: income artificially attributed to a "foreign base," i.e. a country other than the country in which the income is actually earned.

But keep your eye on the big picture. If the CFC actually earns its income in the country in which it is chartered, then it has no Subpart F income, and its earnings are taxed to its U.S. shareholders only if and when those earnings are actually distributed to the shareholders. Moreover, if the more than 50% of the shares of the foreign corporation are not owned by "U.S. shareholders," then the corporation is not a CFC in the first place, in which case the earnings of the corporation are not taxed to the U.S. shareholders until actually distributed to them as dividends.[4]

IV. An Even Briefer Overview of the Foreign Tax Credit

The CFC rules are designed to assure that a foreign business pays tax on its foreign income to at least one taxing jurisdiction, either the U.S. or the foreign country if the foreign country is a taxing jurisdiction and not a tax haven. The foreign tax credit ("FTC") is the principal device in the tax code to assure that a U.S. business pays tax to no more than one country on the same income. The FTC is very important for IJVs.

At its core, the FTC is simple and straightforward. If a U.S. taxpayer pays income tax to a foreign government resulting from its foreign operations, the U.S. taxpayer receives a dollar-for-dollar credit on its U.S. taxes for that year.

> *Example #1*: ABC Corp., a California corporation, operates a retail store in Guatemala. In 2013 it had $10,000,000 in sales in Guatemala for which it paid $1,000,000 to the local tax collector.
> ABC Corp. is entitled to a $1,000,000 tax credit on its U.S. corporate tax return for that year.

It sounds straightforward, but there is a catch. ABC Corp. is still liable to taxation on its worldwide income. As a result, if Guatemala taxes incomes at a lower rate than the

---

[4] If the foreign corporation is a CFC but has no Subpart F Income, the U.S. shareholders must nevertheless disclose their holdings on IRS Form 5471.

U.S. corporate tax rate (which is highly likely) ABC Corp. will receive a FTC for the Guatemala taxes it paid, and will pay the balance to the IRS. But if Guatemala imposes income tax at a higher rate than the U.S. corporate tax, then ABC Corp. will obtain a FTC for the Guatemala tax it paid, but will still have to pay the full tax imposed by Guatemala. The result is that ABC Corp. will wind up paying corporate tax at the higher Guatemala rate.

The principal planning issue with respect to IJVs is who and what qualifies for the FTC, i.e. what foreign taxes are *creditable*, a term whose only existence is with respect to the FTC. For starters, in order to qualify for the FTC, the foreign tax must be an *income tax*, as that term is defined in U.S. – not foreign – tax law. A U.S. income tax is a tax imposed on net income, i.e. business gross income less allowable business deductions. Any other type of tax, regardless of what the foreign government calls it, does not qualify for the FTC, i.e. it is not *creditable*.

> *Example #2*: Country X imposes an "income tax" under a formula that measures the gross sales, payroll expense and rent expense of every local business.
> Although styled as an income tax, it is not an income tax under U.S. tax law and hence does not qualify for the FTC.

As a result, many of the more common taxes imposed by foreign governments, such as sales taxes, VAT taxes and property taxes, although deductible when paid as ordinary business expenses, do not qualify for the FTC.

Another significant limitation on the FTC is that only the party who actually pays the foreign tax may qualify for the FTC. This is a problem in the usual case where the business that pays the foreign tax is a local subsidiary, but the business that needs the FTC is the U.S. parent.

> *Example #3*: ABC Guatemala is a wholly-owned subsidiary of ABC Corp., a California corporation. ABC Guatemala pays income tax to Guatemala. ABC Guatemala is entitled to a FTC. ABC Corp. is not.

The Internal Revenue Code provides a partial fix to this conundrum, viz., the "deemed paid" FTC, which allows the U.S. parent corporation to claim a FTC on the foreign tax paid by its subsidiary. However, the deemed paid FTC can be claimed only as part of the dividend that the subsidiary actually pays to the parent that is attributable to its earnings in that country. Significantly, if there is no dividend, there is no "deemed paid" FTC. In addition, a corporate shareholder of a foreign corporation qualifies for the deemed paid credit only if it owns 10% or more of the stock of the foreign subsidiary. S Corporations, regular corporations (a/k/a "C" corporations) owning less than 10% of the stock of the foreign corporation and all individual shareholders do not qualify. Thus, a U.S. corporation owning all of the stock of its subsidiary will qualify for the deemed paid FTC. But Mr. Jones, a U.S. investor, will not qualify for the deemed paid FTC.

V.　　Check the Tax Treaty

We recently received a call from a client of long standing who advised us that he and a partner were going into business in Austria. They were pretty far along in the planning, having located a production facility to manufacture the industrial fasteners for which they had obtained a patent application. They had even trademarked a name and a design. Our client was calling to ask about the tax ramifications of the proposed business.

Our answer to these telephone inquiries is usually the same: "We don't know. Has anyone checked the U.S.-Austria tax treaty?" There was a silence emanating from the other end of line. The silence gave the answer.

One of the first steps whenever any U.S. business contemplates doing business abroad is to review the tax treaty that the U.S. has entered into with that foreign country. That's *if* the U.S. has entered into such a treaty. The U.S. has entered into bilateral tax treaties with scores of foreign countries, but there are some notable omissions. The U.S. has no tax treaty with such major trading partners as Brazil, Argentina and Taiwan. (For political reasons, we are not likely to ever have a tax treaty with Taiwan.)

But where we do have a tax treaty with a foreign country, the principal purpose of the tax treaty is to define which party to the treaty may – and which may not – tax certain income. This is crucial because, as we have seen, the U.S. may (absent a treaty to the contrary) tax the worldwide income of all U.S. taxpayers. In addition, many tax treaties reduce the rate of tax (or eliminate all taxes) that a country may impose on certain income earned in that country. There are plenty of planning opportunities to be had (and pitfalls to be avoided) in every tax treaty.

Central to any bilateral tax treaty is the concept of the *permanent establishment*, a concept that exists only in tax treaties. Generally, if a business has a permanent establishment (as defined in that particular treaty) in that country, the country in which the permanent establishment is located will be permitted to tax the income from the permanent establishment, and the other treaty country will not tax that income. Importantly, most tax treaties spell out which activities do not constitute a permanent establishment. For example, the U.S.-Thailand tax treaty contains the following provision:

> "...the term 'permanent establishment' shall be deemed <u>not</u> to include:
>
>   a) the use of facilities solely for the purpose of storage or display of goods or merchandise belonging to the enterprise;
>   b) the maintenance of a stock of goods or merchandise belonging to the enterprise solely for the purpose of storage or display;
>   c) the maintenance of a stock of goods or merchandise belonging to the enterprise solely for the purpose of processing by another enterprise;
>   d) the maintenance of a fixed place of business solely for the purpose of purchasing goods or merchandise, or of collecting information, for the enterprise;
>   e) the maintenance of a fixed place of business solely for the purpose of carrying on, for the enterprise, any other activity of a preparatory or auxiliary character."[5]

If a U.S. business conducts operations in Thailand and can limit its activities in Thailand to the excluded activities, the U.S. business will not be subject to Thai

---

[5] Art. 5 of the U.S.-Thailand tax treaty.

income taxation on its Thai operations. Moreover, as we have seen, if the activities are actually conducted in Thailand and there are no non-arm's length purchases or sales, if the Thailand business is a wholly-owned subsidiary of a U.S. corporation, the Thailand corporation will be a CFC, but the CFC will have no Subpart F income. As a result, the parent corporation will be taxed on its Thailand operations only if, as and when the subsidiary distributes a dividend to the U.S. parent.

VI.   Structuring the IJV – Partnership or Corporation?

The most basic – and most important – decision that the U.S. partner in an IJV will need to make is whether the foreign business entity is a partnership or a corporation. As difficult as this decision often is with respect to domestic businesses, it is infinitely more difficult with respect to foreign entities.

For starters, the foreign jurisdiction will likely not even have "corporations" or "partnerships" at all, but a potpourri of strange-sounding entities that may or may not correspond to what we in the U.S. understand to be corporations and partnerships. For example, if the IJV will be located in Germany, will it be an *Aktiengesellschaft* or a *Gessellschaft mit beschraenker Haftung* ("GmbH"), or something else? Needless to say, it is foolhardy to attempt to traverse this minefield without the assistance of knowledgeable local counsel. And let's not forget that the decision whether or not the foreign entity will be corporation or a partnership should be made from a U.S. – not foreign – point of view.

A.   Partnership or Corporation –
General Tax Principles

An IJV that elects to be taxed as a partnership for U.S. tax purposes will be taxed in much the same fashion as a domestic partnership, i.e. the partnership will be a "pass-through" entity, with the partnership itself not subject to tax and the partners subject to tax on their allocable shares of partnership income and loss. If, as is often the case, the venture expects to incur losses in the first year or years of operation, operating in partnership form will result in the U.S. being able to use the IJV's losses against its U.S. or other foreign income. If the IJV is taxed as a corporation, the losses cannot be allocated to the U.S. parent.

Conversely, if the IJV is taxed as a partnership and it generates profits, the U.S. partner will be subject to immediate taxation on its share of the profits, whether those profits are distributed or not, with no ability to defer the incidence of tax. If the IJV is taxed as a corporation, the U.S. parent has the ability to defer the U.S. tax by not distributing the profits, assuming, of course, that the profits do not constitute the Subpart F income of a CFC. The ability to defer U.S. taxes is illusory, however, if the local government will subject the IJV to its own corporate taxes at rates that are as high or almost as high as the U.S. corporate tax rate.

If, however, the U.S. partner has unused foreign tax credits, it could use those credits to directly offset the profits allocated to it by the IJV. It would be able to use the foreign tax credits if the IJV were taxed as a corporation, and would be limited to the "deemed" foreign tax credit. Finally, if in the rare case that the U.S. partner is an individual or an S corporation, partnership taxation might be preferable (it least from a tax standpoint), because an individual or an S corporation does not qualify for the "deemed" foreign tax credit.

This discussion should make it clear that with respect to the most basic decision regarding how the IJV should be taxed, one size definitely does not fit all.

B.   Limited and Unlimited Liability

No one wants to be sued. But if you are going to become a defendant in a lawsuit, you would much prefer to be sued in Tarzana, California than in Tanzania. Moreover, if your assets are to be placed at risk as a result of your foreign operations, you would prefer that you be held liable only for your own wrongdoing, which you have the ability to control, and not the wrongdoing of a business partner, which you have less ability to control.

Just as in the U.S., some forms of foreign business ownership provide more limitation from liability than others. If limited liability is a goal – and it should be – one of the first goals is to choose the form of foreign ownership that provides the most insulation from creditor claims.

Every U.S. state permits the formation within that state of a limited liability company, which provides not only for the limited liability of the owners (the "members") of the LLC, but also provides the substantial tax benefit of being a tax partnership and therefore a "pass-through" entity for tax purposes. As such, the LLC is not considered a taxpayer at all. Instead the owners are taxed on their proportionate share of the LLC's profits, and are allocated their share of the LLC's losses, if any. In that respect, an LLC is most closely analogous to a U.S. corporation that elects to be treated as an "S" corporation. If a domestic corporation elects "S" status, the corporation itself is not a taxpayer; the shareholders pay their proportionate shares of the taxes of the corporation's earnings. Nevertheless, the shareholders have the same limited liability as the shareholders in a "regular" or "C" corporation.

Not all countries provide for entities that are analogous to U.S. LLC's. Surprisingly, neither the Canadian federal government, which permits incorporation of federal entities, nor any of the Canadian provinces, provide for the formation of an LLC or anything like it, viz., an entity that is a pass-through for tax purposes but which provides limited liability for all of its owners. The closest thing that Canada has to our LLC is a limited partnership, which provides for limited liability for the limited partners, but which renders the general partner liable for all of the entity's debts and liabilities.

C.   "Check the Box" and "Per Se" Corporations

To a certain extent, the IRS is fairly generous with the respect to your choice of entity. The IRS will allow you to determine whether you wish your IJV to be treated for U.S. tax purposes as a corporation or as a partnership. You make the election by checking a box on IRS Form 8832 (*see exhibit C)* and filing the form with the IRS. An example of the form is provided in the appendix of this book. It's that simple. Of course, checking the box will have no effect on how the local taxing authority will tax the entity, which will be determined under local law and on the presence or absence of a tax treaty between the U.S. and the local country. Checking the box does, however, provide you with certainty as to how the U.S. will tax the IJV.

The IRS publishes a list of foreign entities that do *not* qualify for the check-the-box election. These are entities that the IRS has determined so closely resemble U.S. corporations that they cannot possibly be taxed as pass-through entities. They are *per se* corporations, and are taxed in the U.S. as corporations. If, for whatever reason, you choose one of these listed entities through which to operate the IJV, you cannot be a pass-through entity for U.S. tax purposes.[6]

Conversely, if a foreign entity is not on the list of *per se* entities, you may elect to treat the entity as a pass-through entity for U.S. tax purposes, even if the entity so closely resembles a corporation that the local government would not treat it as a pass-through entity under its own tax law. If the entity is not on the list of *per se* corporations and the entity has only one owner (which will be the case if the entity is a wholly-owned subsidiary of a U.S. parent), the entity will be treated as a *disregarded entity* for U.S. tax purposes. All of the income, gains, profits and losses allocated and distributed to the foreign subsidiary will be deemed to be that of the parent for U.S. tax purposes. If the entity has more than one owner, the entity will be treated as a partnership for U.S. tax purposes, unless it makes an election to be taxed as a corporation.

If the "check the box" election is available, the decision whether to elect to have the foreign entity be treated as a pass-through entity or taxed as a corporation is of critical importance. If it is contemplated that the entity will incur losses in its initial year or years of operation, it would be beneficial to elect pass-through treatment so as to enable the U.S. parent to claim the foreign losses. On the

---

[6] The list appears in Treasury Regulation §301.7701-3(a).

other hand, there is no opportunity for deferral if the foreign entity is a pass-through; foreign income will be taxed to the parent as received. If, however, the foreign entity elects to be taxed as a corporation, and the foreign entity is either not a CFC or is a CFC but does not have Subpart F income, then the U.S. parent will have the ability to control the timing of the taxation of its foreign income by timing the distributions of dividends from the foreign entity to the parent.

VII.   Transfers of Assets to a Foreign IJV

As a general rule, the transfer of appreciated assets to a corporation in exchange for the stock of the corporation is not an event resulting in U.S. taxation. The same is generally true of transfers of assets to partnerships. People form corporations and partnerships every day, transferring equipment, inventory, cash and intellectual property to the corporation or the partnership and never give it a second thought. They certainly do not think that these transactions result in taxes, and generally they're correct in this assumption.

The transfer of appreciated assets to a foreign corporation or partnership, however, offers the opportunity for tax avoidance. For example, if Mr. Jones, a U.S. citizen, owns appreciated corporate stock, the sale of that stock would undoubtedly result in U.S. capital gains taxes. If, however, Mr. Jones were to transfer the stock to a foreign corporation in exchange for shares of the foreign corporation, and the foreign corporation were to sell the stock, Mr. Jones might be able to avoid – or at least defer – the tax on the sale.

Section 367 of the Internal Revenue Code is designed to prevent this form of tax abuse. It provides that the contribution of appreciated assets to a foreign corporation *is* subject to tax, as if the contribution were a taxable sale. However, §367 contains an important exception: There is no tax imposed on the transfer of assets to the foreign corporation if the foreign corporation uses the contributed assets in a foreign trade or business. This exception is usually sufficient to cover the common scenario involving the transfer of assets to an IJV that will be used in the IJV's foreign operations.

There is, however, an important "exception to the exception" contained in §367(d). If *intangible assets* are contributed to a foreign corporation or foreign partnership, the contribution is treated as the sale of the intangibles in exchange for a *royalty*, and that hypothetical annual royalty is subject to U.S. tax. The amount of the royalty is computed based upon the foreign corporation or partnership's income attributable to the intangible assets. The rationale for this "exception to the exception" is to prevent a U.S. taxpayer from taking deductions attributable to the costs of developing the intangible asset, and then deferring the income resulting from that intangible. For the purposes of §367, "intangibles" includes the usual suspects such as trademarks and patents, franchises and licenses. It does not, however, include goodwill.

There is an easy way to avoid the sting of §367(d), but only if the IJV is taxed as a partnership for U.S. tax purposes. The IJV will be entitled to a deduction for the royalty it is deemed to have paid. If the partnership agreement allocates the entire deduction to the U.S. partner (it is not likely the foreign partner will have any need of it), the deduction will offset the income.

Any U.S. person who owns 10% or more of a foreign partnership must report the transfer of assets to the foreign partnership on Form 8865 (*see Exhibit D*). The penalties for failure to do are onerous in the extreme: 10% of the fair market value of the property transferred and treatment of the transferred property as if it were a taxable sale, up to a maximum of $100,000 if the failure to file was unintentional. There is no maximum if the failure to file was deemed to be intentional.

VIII. Can an S Corporation Ever be a Partner in an IJV?

It doesn't happen often, but there are occasions when a U.S. "S" corporation desires to engage in an IJV. An "S" corporation may be a partner in an IJV. Here's how.

An "S" corporation may not have a corporate shareholder. With some unimportant exceptions, all of the "S" corporation's shareholders must be U.S. individuals. The presence of a single foreign shareholder, or one corporate shareholder, will disqualify the entity as an "S" corporation for all of the shareholders. Moreover, an S corporation may not be part of an "affiliated group" of corporations, i.e. it cannot own a corporate subsidiary.

There is, however, one important exception to this rule: An "S" corporation may own a "Qualified S Corporation Subsidiary," universally known as a "QSub." To qualify, the "S" corporation must own all of the stock of the QSub, which must be a domestic corporation. If these requirements are met, the QSub is treated as an invisible entity for U.S. tax purposes. All of the QSub's assets and liabilities are treated as owned by its parent, the "S" corporation. All of the gains, profits and losses allocated to the QSub are treated as being the gains, profits and losses of the "S" corporation.

The QSub may be an invisible entity for U.S. income tax purposes, but it is very real for all other purposes. For liability purposes, the QSub interposes a level of insulation between the local operating entity and the U.S. "S" corporation owner. If and to the extent local law or taxing authorities require disclosure of the parent of the local partner of IJV, that parent is the QSub, not the "S" corporation.

The manner in which a U.S. "S" corporation should engage in an IJV is as follows:

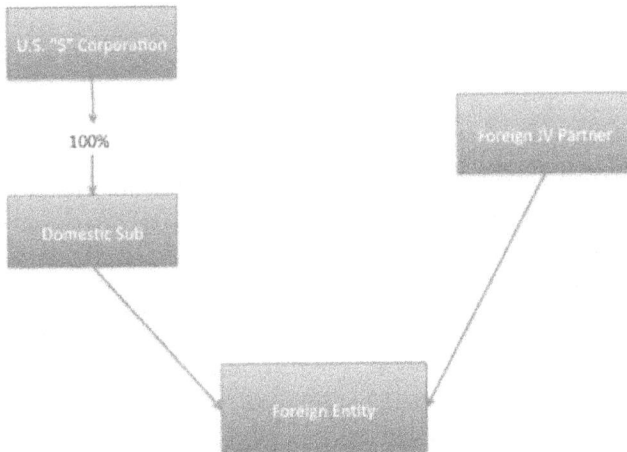

Figure 1

"S" Corporations in IJV's suffer one disability that "C" corporations do not. An "S" corporation does not qualify for the "deemed" foreign tax credit. As a result, if the local entity pays local income taxes, the U.S. "S" corporation parent will be limited to a deduction on its own tax return with respect to the local taxes that the IJV paid. It will not be able to claim a credit.

IX.   Tax-Efficient Structuring

A.   Operate Through a Local Branch?

For many U.S. businesses desiring to operate abroad, the option exists to not enter into an IJV at all, but to simply engage in business operations in the foreign country through a local branch. We *always* advise our clients to avoid operating through a local branch, for reasons having nothing to do with taxes. If a U.S. business conducts business directly in a foreign country, there is no avoiding the jurisdiction of the local courts. Anyone can bring a lawsuit in the local country alleging anything, and the assets of the U.S. business will be exposed.

There is also little to recommend operating through a local branch from a tax perspective. The local country will undoubtedly subject the operations of the local branch to taxation on its local income. Moreover, the U.S. will also tax the profits of the foreign branch. As we have seen, U.S. corporations are subject to tax on their world-wide income. It is possible that this result will be mitigated by a tax treaty between the U.S. and the local country. If there is no tax treaty, the U.S. corporation may qualify for the direct foreign tax credit. But the best result this achieves is only one level of taxation at U.S. regular corporate rates, with no ability to defer the payment of tax.

B.   Operating as an IJV

Let's take a look at the most basic form of IJV from a tax perspective. Let's assume that Friendly, Inc. is a U.S. corporation. It forms an IJV in Italy with Local, its Italian partner. The IJV forms "F-L Partners" in Italy, with Friendly and Local being equal partners. Let's further assume that the entity Friendly and Local have selected is not a *per se* corporation, permitting Friendly, Inc. to "check the box" and treat the entity as a partnership for U.S. tax purposes, which it does.

The structure of F-L Partners is shown on Figure 2.

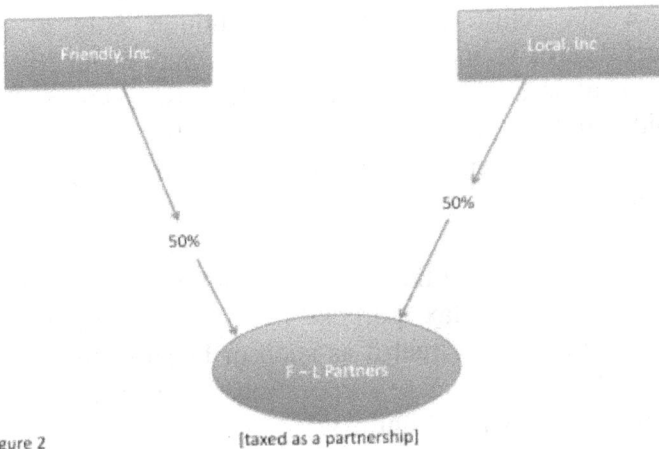

Figure 2   [taxed as a partnership]

The principal tax advantage to Friendly is that it provides a flow-through of partnership profits and losses directly to Friendly. To the extent that F-L pays local income taxes, Friendly will qualify for the direct foreign tax credit on its share of F-L's taxes, without the necessity of a dividend if it were limited to the deemed foreign tax credit.

The principal tax disadvantage to Friendly is that this structure provides Friendly with no ability to defer the incidence of tax. Friendly will be taxed on its allocable share of F-L's income, whether the cash is distributed to it or not.

There is another possible disadvantage, depending on the tax law of the country in which the IJV conducts business. If the IJV is taxed locally as a pass-through entity, it is possible that the taxing authority will treat every partner in the IJV as being engaged in a local business, which may result in the foreign partner in the IJV being required to file a local tax return with the taxing authority. In the above example, that would require Friendly, Inc. to file a tax return in Italy, even though only a small percentage of its income and/or profits may result from the IJV. That is a result that most U.S. businesses prefer to avoid, and which can be avoided by interposing a subsidiary between itself and the entity that acts as the local partner.

Let's assume that F-L were treated as a corporation for U.S. income tax purposes, either because Friendly checked the box to treat it as such or because the entity is on the IRS' list of *per se* corporations. The structure of F-L Partners is shown on Figure 3.

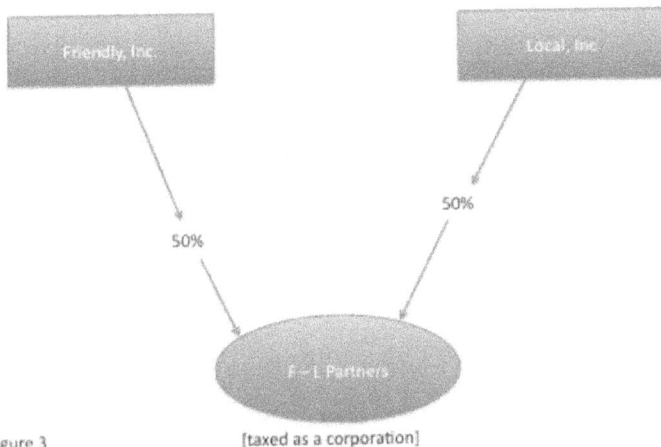

Figure 3   [taxed as a corporation]

The structure looks the same, but the results are very different. F-L is taxed as a corporation, but since Friendly owns only 50% of F-L, F-L cannot be a CFC. As a result, the U.S. cannot tax the operations of F-L and it cannot tax Friendly's distributive share of F-L's earnings. Thus, Friendly has achieved a level of deferral of its foreign income that was not possible had F-L been taxed as a partnership. How much of a deferral Friendly has achieved will depend upon if and when F-L declares and pays a dividend. Friendly will be taxed on any dividends it receives from F-L.

With some fairly sophisticated planning, we can achieve the best of all worlds. Let us assume that, as in Figure 2, F-L Partners may elect to be taxed as a partnership. But instead of Friendly being the 50% partner of F-L, Friendly forms a corporation, "Holding, Inc." in a low or no-tax jurisdiction, and Holding becomes the 50% partner in F-L. The structure is shown in Figure 4.

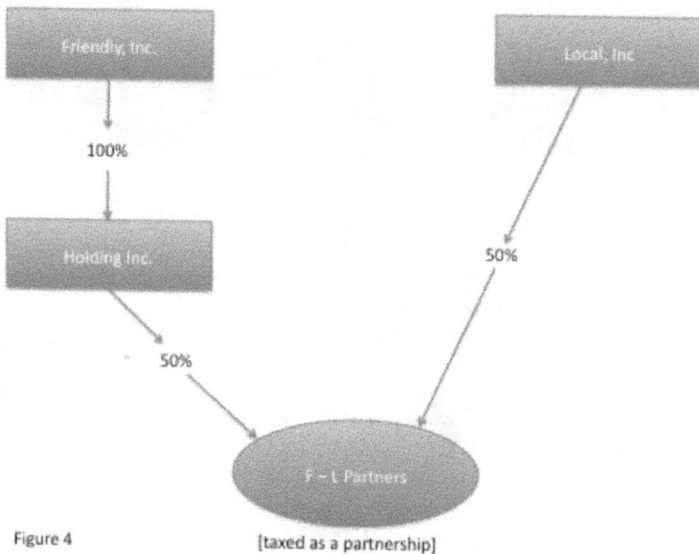

Figure 4   [taxed as a partnership]

In this structure, Friendly has achieved the best of all worlds. Because F-L is taxed as a partnership for U.S. income tax purposes, it is a pass-through entity. But Friendly is not immediately taxed on the income that is allocated to it, because it has not received the income; Holding does, and Holding pays little or no tax on the income it receives from F-L, having been chartered in a tax haven. Only when Holding distributes its income to its parent – Friendly – will Friendly be subject to tax on the distributions. In the interim, Holding can apply its earnings to other foreign investments or business operations on a pre-tax basis.

The structure outlined in Figure 4 works fine if F-L generates profits. It does not work so well if F-L generates losses, because the losses will be trapped in Holding. In order to assure that an IJV's losses can be allocated to and used by the U.S. parent, we recommend the formation of a *foreign disregarded entity* (Sub #1) to act as the partner in the IJV. This structure is outlined in Figure 5:

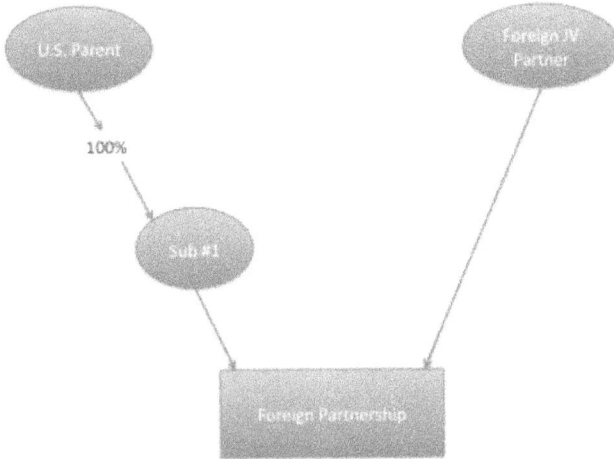

Figure 5

Since Sub #1 has only one owner, it may "check the box" by electing (on Form 8832) to be a disregarded entity for U.S. tax purposes (*see Exhibit C*). That means that IJV losses that are allocable to the U.S. parent will flow directly through to the U.S. parent. However, Sub #1 is a disregarded entity only for U.S. income tax purposes. It is very real for all other purposes. If there are lawsuits in the local country involving the IJV's operations, it is likely that Sub #1 – not its U.S. parent – will be the defendant. More importantly, it is Sub #1 – not the U.S. parent – whose assets are at risk with respect to whatever claims arise in the local country.

If the IJV allocates profits to its partners, the U.S. parent will be able to claim the direct foreign tax credit, for a simple reason that Sub #1 is a disregarded entity. For purposes of the FTC, the U.S. parent – not Sub #1 – is deemed to have paid the local tax, making it eligible for the direct FTC.

All of the foregoing should reveal one truism: When it comes to structuring the IJV, one size definitely does not fit all. Some IJV's anticipate profits in their early years of operations; others anticipate losses. Some IJV's will never be CFC's because the foreign partners will own 50% or more of the local entity. Some IJV's that are CFC's will never generate Subpart F income. Some countries permit the formation of entities that are pass-through entities; others do not. Every IJV is unique.

Chapter 4: Negotiating the Joint Venture Agreement

I.   Introduction

Let's assume that you have found your prospective joint venture partner. You have performed all of the due diligence you can possibly perform of both the country in which the IJV will operate and your prospective partner itself. All of the signs point to the potential for a profitable IJV.

Now the hard work begins. Before any more money, time and energy is expended in this venture, a binding agreement *must* be finalized that, to the greatest extent, expresses every aspect of the operations of the IJV and leaves as little as possible to chance. There will always be issues that arise that no one contemplated or discussed. But the most successful IJV's minimize the unknowns by attempting to negotiate and reduce to writing as many of the deal points as possible. If there are material points that cannot be reconciled during the negotiations, it is not likely they will be resolved once the business gets going. At a minimum, *never, ever, ever enter into an IJV without first signing a definitive, binding joint venture agreement*!

We have had clients who wince when we attempt to enforce this rule. There are cultures where trust – not contracts -- is paramount. Our clients have expressed to us a concern that an insistence on a signed definitive IJV agreement is a sign that we don't trust our foreign partner, who will be offended by our insistence that everything be documented in advance. When a client expresses this concern, our advice is always the same: Make us the bad guy. We advise our client to inform his counterpart that his hands are tied, and that his lawyer will not let the deal close unless all of his requirements are met. Our client may need to retain the goodwill and friendship of his partner going forward. We don't.

But we are getting ahead of ourselves. Before there is a signed IJV agreement, there should be a *letter of intent* (*see Exhibit A*).

II.   The Letter of Intent

Every binding IJV agreement should be preceded with a *nonbinding* letter of intent. Usually, the LOI is what it says it is, a letter, addressed from one of the partners to the other. Ideally, an LOI should be as short as possible, running to no more than two or three pages. The LOI should spell out, in plain language with as little legalese as possible, the main points of the prospective IJV. I prefer to phrase an LOI to make it clear that it is a nonbinding expression of all of the important deal points, and that it contemplates the signing of a definitive, binding IJV agreement. The last thing you want to happen is for your partner to assume that once he signs the LOI all of the drafting has been done and the IJV is ready to go into business.

Here is a short checklist of all of the items that should be expressed in an LOI:

• *The exact names of the IJV partners*. This may sound obvious, but it anything but. If you (or your partner) will not be the JV partner, but if instead you will form a local or domestic subsidiary to act as the JV partner, you can obviate a lot of grief by informing your partner that your U.S. corporation will not be his partner, and that a newly-formed entity, formed for the purpose of entering into the IJV will be the JV partner. This fact should have been expressed when the parties were negotiating the deal that lead to the LOI, but often it is not, especially if management negotiated the deal without the presence of the lawyers.

• *The exact name and address of the IJV*. If the IJV will be conducted in a country that is not English-speaking, it may be important to come to an understanding regarding the name under which the IJV will operate. This is especially true if the IJV will market products or services that will bear the name of the IJV. The local jurisdiction may have a say in what the IJV is called. For example, the province of Quebec has very strict rules regarding bilingualism, requiring every entity to have a French-name equivalent. If the IJV will operate under a different name in the local country, it is wise to check to see if that name is available, especially if the IJV will operate in third countries.

• *A short description of the business of the IJV*. This may require only a sentence or two. If the partners have different ideas about what business the IJV will be engaged in, it would be nice to discern that fact sooner rather than later.

• *A short description of the duties of each partner*. Once again, this should require only one or two sentences.

• *A short description of the capital contributions of each partner*. It is important to express not only the initial capital contributions of each partner, but any additional capital contributions that may be required in the future, as well as the consequences for failure to make a capital contribution.

• *A description of the rights of the partners to distributions of income and cash*. It is important that each party understand not only the percentage of profit that each partner will be entitled to receive, but the timing thereof.

It should be obvious by now that the principal advantage of the LOI is to reveal differences that are so fundamental that if not resolved it will not be possible to ever enter into a definitive agreement. If ferocious negotiations break out over the wording of the LOI, it's likely that a definitive agreement – and an IJV – is a pipe dream. But it's better to learn that you will not be able to get to "yes" earlier rather than later.

A properly drafted LOI will make it abundantly clear that the LOI is *non-binding*, that it is merely an expression of the parties' present intent to continue negotiating a binding agreement. The last thing you want to have happen is for the negotiations to break down and then find yourself being sued because you allegedly breached a binding agreement. This happens in cases where the negotiations break down and one party then enters into an IJV or other arrangement with another suitor.

There are, however, one or two provisions in an LOI that you may wish to be binding, i.e. to be legally enforceable. You may wish to include a binding provision in the LOI that provides that both the contents of the LOI and the fact of the LOI itself will be kept confidential, and will not be disclosed to anyone except those parties who need to know of the LOI, which includes your attorneys, accountants, investment bankers and possibly one or two key employees. The LOI should state that it has a definite (usually short) term during which each party will use its best efforts to negotiate a binding agreement. During that term, each party should be prevented from "shopping" the LOI, i.e. trying to get a better deal with someone else.

The second provision that should be binding is a *non-disclosure covenant,* which is sometimes expressed in the LOI but is often expressed in a separate document. Both parties to an IJV will likely disclose confidential information to the other about their respective business operations during the course of negotiations. If the negotiations fail and no IJV is formed, it might be harmful to your business if pricing data, secret formulae, customer and supplier arrangements and a host of other sensitive information is left floating around for all to see. The LOI (or a stand-alone non-disclosure agreement) should contain a binding provision that describes all of the proprietary information that will be shared during the term of the LOI and which requires each party to the LOI to return to the other any documents containing confidential information that were provided during the LOI term in the event that the LOI does not lead to a binding IJV agreement.

Everyone knows that, where the parties to an agreement reside in different countries that may be oceans apart, binding contractual provisions may be very difficult (impossible?) to enforce. Nevertheless, it is important that each side realizes that the other is serious about keeping proprietary information out of the hands of competitors or potential competitors. The non-disclosure aspects of the LOI should be discussed before the LOI is signed. If you sense that your potential partner is cavalier about trade secrets, you may have smoked out a potential problem that needs to be addressed.

A template of a non-binding letter of intent is attached as Attachment A.

III. Do Not Commit Cash until the Definitive Agreement Has Been Signed

We often learn – to our horror – that our client has made what is sometimes a substantial cash commitment before the definitive IJV has been signed. There seems to be as many reasons for this as there are instances of it occurring. For example, the IJV may contemplate that a new plant will be leased, and that the U.S. partner will provide the cash to secure the lease. The prospective partner then informs my client that the location has been found, but that the funds necessary to secure the lease must be wired to the lessor *by tomorrow* or the lease will be lost to someone else. My client then bites the bullet and wires the cash. If no IJV is ever formed, my client is out the wired funds. But that is not the worst part. Having already made a cash commitment to an IJV that has not been finalized, the negotiating strengths and weaknesses have now undergone a subtle change. My client's negotiating position has been weakened, and the local partner's negotiating position has been strengthened. If my client has committed enough cash, my client may feel that he must conclude the IJV, in which case he has no negotiating leverage. I once had a client who completely retooled his manufacturing plant in anticipation of an IJV that had not yet been fully negotiated. Needless to say, we had no negotiating leverage whatever.

IV. The Tasks and Responsibilities Spreadsheet

Like many attorneys, we strongly favor the preparation of a spreadsheet that neatly and clearly lays out who will do what and when. If all parties agree to a "T&R" it has the effect of focusing everyone on the tasks at hand.

We are not always successful in getting the parties to agree to a T&R, but we never stop trying.

A T&R has three columns: the task that needs to be performed, the identity of the person who will perform the task, and the due date by which the task should be performed. For example, if Mr. Singh, a local lawyer in India, is charged with the responsibility of registering the entity through which the IJV will be operating with the local registrar of companies, that fact is described in the spreadsheet:

T&R	Responsible Person(s)	Due Date
Register company	Singh	8/31/13

The preparation of the T&R requires everyone to focus on all of the matters that need to be performed. Once finalized, both parties to the IJV, their lawyers, accountants, investment bankers (if any) and key personnel will all have a copy of the T&R, and everyone checks off the items as they are performed. Generally, no one wants to be exposed as the party who is not pulling his oar. The T&R gets everyone – including Mr. Singh -- to focus.

V. The Terms of the Binding IJV Agreement

Let us assume that a non-binding LOI has been signed. The LOI states that each party will use its best efforts to finalize a binding IJV agreement by the end of the term of the LOI. I prefer to have a term that is not longer than 180 days. If the term of the LOI is too short, finalizing an agreement before the end of the term is simply impossible, and the parties will be required to negotiate an extension of the LOI term. If the term is too long, people tend to put it off for other work that is more pressing. My experience tells me that if an agreement cannot be reached in 180 days, it likely never will.

It is possible that your prospective IJV partner may question the need for involving teams of lawyers and accountants in order to conclude an IJV agreement. In many cultures, trust is paramount, and your prospective partner may express his concern that you don't trust him and that the definitive agreement is being used as a substitute for trust. At that point, you must make it clear to your prospective partner that there is no substitute for trust, but that we value written agreements very highly in that the written agreement, that spells out both parties' understanding on as many issues as possible, will reduce the chances of misunderstandings once the IVJ has commenced operations.

With that in mind, let's examine all of the matters that should be included in the definitive agreement:

• *The jurisdiction of the IJV, and its legal status.* We can assume that the IJV will be formed in the local country. It is likely that it will be an entity that is registered with either the local city or province or with the national government. In some countries (e.g. Canada) you have a choice as to whether to register with the local government or with the national government. If such an option exists, I prefer that the decision be made following consultation with our local counsel.

A technical issue arises with respect to choice of entity right from the start. An entity may be treated under local law as a separate entity, and provide its owners with limited liability. It may or may not be a pass-through entity for local tax purposes. Nevertheless, as we saw in Chapter

IV, unless a local entity appears on the list of "per se" corporations in Treasury Regulation §301.7701-3(a), a U.S. owner of the entity has the option to treat the local entity as a "pass-through" entity for U.S. tax purposes, even if it is not a pass-through entity under local law. If the U.S. partner intends to elect to treat the local entity as a pass-through entity for U.S. tax purposes, that fact should be disclosed in the agreement.

• *The name of IJV, and the identities of the partners.* The name of the IJV will have been disclosed in the letter of intent. If the IJV will operate under one name in one language and another name in another language, that fact must of course be disclosed.

The parties to an IJV often overlook the issue of the *ownership* of the name. If the IJV will sell its products or services under a branded name, the parties should have a clear understanding as to whether the name and the associated trademarks, logos, domain names, etc. will be owned by the IJV itself or by one of the partners. In the section of the agreement that deals with the termination of the IJV, mention should be made regarding the ownership of this intellectual property upon the termination of the IJV.

The identities of the parties will likely also have been mentioned in the letter of intent. But not always. If you have decided that your participation in the IJV will be through a local or foreign subsidiary, the identity of the subsidiary should also be disclosed.

• *The purpose and scope of the IJV.* In order to obviate misunderstandings and conflicts later on, it is important to clearly define the purpose of the IJV. For example, if the purpose of the IJV is to manufacture and sell a certain line of industrial fasteners, the agreement should state that fact. If, however, the local production facility permits the manufacture of nails and screws for the retail public, an issue arises as to whether the IJV may manufacture and sell this second line as well. A more delicate issue arises if your local partner wishes to use the local plant, as well as the labor force committed to the IJV, to manufacture and sell items that are not contemplated by the IJV. If this possibility exists, it should be addressed during the negotiations leading up to the agreement, not after.

Just as important as the purpose of the IJV is its scope. If the agreement contemplates that the IJV will its products only in the local market, the agreement should provide that the IJV will not sell its products out of the local market without the consent of both partners. If sales in the local market are successful, your local partner might wish to expand sales to other markets. You might be willing to so that, provided that you do not already sell into that market, in which event your own IJV would be a competitor. Even if you do not sell into a third market, you might not wish the IJV to do so. For example, the products manufactured in the local market may be inferior in quality to the products you sell in other markets, and you might not wish to dilute your brand by selling the products manufactured by the IJV in third countries. Conversely, if sales to third countries are permitted, does the IJV contemplate that your existing distribution network will be used to facilitate sales in the third countries? If so, your agreement relative to the division of profits for sales in the local country might not work for sales into third countries.

• *Initial and Subsequent Capital Contributions.* It is often the case that the local partner contributes plant, equipment and labor to the IJV and the U.S. partner contributes cash. But not always. If it is the case that each party is required to contribute cash to the IJV, that requirement must be spelled out.

A more problematical issue is the requirement – if any -- for the contribution of additional funds. The local partner may simply not have the ability to contribute any more funds, relying on the U.S. partner to foot all of the bills. If that is the case, the U.S. partner who is required to contribute additional capital may then wish to have the rights to IJV profits amended to reflect the altered ratio of capital contributions, something the local partner might resist. Once again, it is important to resolve this issue in the drafting of the agreement rather than sweeping it under the rug until it arises after the IJV has been formed.

If the IJV contemplates that the local partner will contribute intellectual property such as trademarks and patents to the IJV, the issue arises as to whether the local partner will contribute the IP to the IJV – so that the IJV will own the IP – or will merely license the IP to the IJV. If the agreement contemplates that the IJV will own IP, then a formal assignment should be prepared and signed contemporaneously with the formation of the IJV. If the local partner will merely license the IP to the IJV, then a license agreement should be prepared. Presumably, the IJV will be the *exclusive* licensee of the IP in the local market, if not worldwide. One of my clients once learned that a particularly important copyright was not actually owned by his potential partner; the partner was himself merely a licensee with no right to sublicense the copyright. It's nice to learn those things before you go into business with a partner, not after.

In addition to the IP that has been developed before the IJV has been formed, it may be important to spell out who will own any improvements and/or refinements to the

IP following the formation of the IJV. Needless to say, if the IJV expends its own funds to develop additional IP, the IJV should own the IP that results from these efforts. But if only one of the partners will be charged with the R&D expense of developing technology during the IJV, only that partner – and not the IJV or the other partner – should have the right to patent the enhanced technology.

The parties should also address the issue of the IJV's debts. Presumably, the IJV will incur its own debts and pay its debts out of its business operations. If and to the extent a partner is required to guarantee its partner's individual debts, that issue must be addressed. It is important that obtain the opinion of your local counsel regarding the extent to which you will be liable for your partner's debts and liabilities under local law, whether or not you are contractually liable for those debts.

• *Management of the IJV.* It is absolutely essential that both the overall management of the IJV its day-to-day management be spelled out in the agreement. The negotiations on this point will reveal assumptions that may not be mutual and items that will require further discussion that should be resolved sooner rather than later.

The most basic issue will be who will have overall authority over the enterprise. If the entity is a corporation (or something akin to it under local law), the body that has the legal responsibility over the entity is the board of directors. If that is the case, the number of persons on the board and each partner's right to appoint persons to the board must be spelled out. If there is a board of directors or something akin to it, its duties must be spelled out. Specifically, the right of the board of directors to hire, fire and determine the compensation and duties of the officers should be delineated in detail.

The IJV will, of course, have local managers, be they designated as officers, managers or something else. The duties of each officer – particularly the president or chief executive officer – should be spelled out in detail. If and to the extent the CEO has the authority to hire and fire other officers and employees, it should be described. If there are limitations of the CEO's authority, i.e. the extent that he must first obtain board of directors' approval, it should also be spelled out. For example, if you do not wish to grant any local manager the authority to enter into any contract or lease that will obligate the IJV in excess of a fixed amount, the agreement should make that fact clear to both partners and the manager. If there are limitations on the ability of the CEO to expend IJV funds for a particular purpose, they should also be described. If it is contemplated that the CEO will be provided with an operating budget, that too should be included in the agreement.

• *Authority over Distributions.* Closely related to issue of management is the issue of the timing of distributions to the partners. This issue is critically important if the U.S. partner has elected to treat the IJV as a pass-through entity for U.S. tax purposes. If so, the U.S. partner will be subject to tax on its share of the IJV's annual profits that have been *allocated* to it, whether those profits have been distributed or not. As a result, the U.S. partner might have profits allocated to it, without the cash to tax on the profits. The agreement must therefore require the CEO or manager of the IJV to make minimum distributions to the partners in order to permit the partners to meet their tax obligations.

The amount and timing of distributions is likely to be important aside from taxes. If the U.S. partner is a well-heeled multinational, it may be amenable to a deferral of distributions, especially if it takes the long view. But the local partner may need distributions as quickly as possible, especially if the local partner has made a substantial investment in the IJV.

These are the essential features of any definitive IJV agreement. There are a number of technical issues that should be included in an IJV agreement, especially if, as is likely, the U.S. partner (or its parent) will be subject to U.S. taxation.

• *Pricing Issues.* The partners may not realize it, but they have a potential conflict of interest with respect to how the IJV will price the products it sells. This potential conflict should be addressed before operations are commenced.

If the products that the IJV will sell in the local market are produced by the U.S. partner in the U.S., or if the components that go into the final product are produced in the U.S., then it will likely be to the U.S. partner's advantage to sell the products and/or the components to the IJV at a relatively low price. This shifts income – and income tax – to the local country. This benefits the U.S. partner, often to the detriment of the local partner. Conversely, if the products are sold to the IJV at their fair market value, this will increase taxable income (and U.S. tax) to the U.S. partner, and will decrease the IJV's taxes in the local market. Needless to say, these pricing issues should be resolved before operations commence.

• *Audit Committee?* This is a very delicate issue. Each partner of the IJV should have the right to audit the financial statements and the financial books of account of the IJV. Each partner should be given the right to delegate to auditors of its choosing the ability to conduct periodic audits. This may raise the eyebrows of your counterparties, but if it does, I like to remind them of President Reagan's oft-quoted mantra, "Trust but Verify."

• *Tax Elections*. If the IJV is taxed is a partnership, or if the U.S. partner desires that the IJV elect to tax the entity as a partnership, then the agreement should specify that the IJV will make the election. The agreement should make the U.S. partner the "Tax Matters Partner" for all U.S. tax purposes, giving the U.S. partner the right to make all U.S. tax elections that are beneficial for U.S. tax purposes.

The U.S. partner will exercise its election to treat the IJV as a partnership by filing Form 8832 (*See Exhibit C)* with the IRS.

• *Foreign Corrupt Practices Act Issues*. As we saw in Chapter III, one of the things you must ascertain before you finalize an IJV is whether your prospective partner has violated either the U.S. Foreign Corrupt Practices Act or its local equivalent, or both. It is wise to include in the agreement a mutual representation that neither party has violated the FCPA and a covenant that neither party will do anything that will violate the FCPA, that either party may terminate the IJV if the other is found to have violated the FCPA, and that if either party to the agreement has any doubt that the FCPA has been violated, the practice or the violation must be promptly reported to the other party.

Remember: You cannot avoid the FCPA by letting your partner commit the violations while you close your eyes, and you cannot avoid FCPA liability by inserting a provision in the agreement where under your partner promises not to violate the FCPA. But inserting such a provision cannot hurt. It shows that you are cognizant of

FCPA issues and have no intent to use your partner to commit FCPA violations.

• *Dispute Resolution*. It is wise to include a provision in the agreement for the resolution of disputes in the event that they arise. It is best to have disputes resolved in a neutral country before a neutral arbitrator such as the International Centre for Dispute Resolution, which is the international arm of the American Arbitration Association. Here is a typical dispute resolution clause.

"In the event of any controversy or claim arising out of or relating to this agreement, or a breach thereof, the parties hereto agree first to try to settle the dispute by mediation, administered by the Inter-national Centre for Dispute Resolution under its Mediation Rules. If settlement is not reached within 60 days after service of a written demand for mediation, any unresolved controversy or claim arising out of or relating to this agreement shall be settled by arbitration in accordance with the International Arbitration Rules of the Inter-national Centre for Dispute Resolution."

• *Whose Law Governs*? The agreement must spell out whether and the extent to which local law (i.e. the law of place where the IJV will operate) will govern, and the extent, if at all, local law will be superseded by U.S. or some country's tax laws. This is not as obvious as it might first appear. A U.S. partner may be stuck with local law in many respects, but not in others, especially local tax law.

EXHIBIT A

International Joint Ventures Letter of Intent

Southern California Kiddie Prints, Inc.
2665 Vernon Avenue
Vernon, CA 93225

November 22, 2013

Leiser GmbH
Boltzmanngasse 16
1090 Vienna
Austria
Attn: Hr. Rolf Heinrich, President

> RE: Southern California Kiddie
> Prints, Inc/Leiser GmbH
> Formation of Joint Venture
> "Wirf den Ball GesmbH"
> Non-Binding Letter of Intent

Dear Hr. Heinrich:

This letter, when executed by yourself on behalf of Leiser GmbH ("Leiser") an entity formed under the laws of Austria, will confirm the understanding that we have already reached and will constitute our non-binding letter of intent to use our mutual best efforts to enter into a binding agreement to form a joint venture under the laws of Austria. The broad outlines of the agreement we have reached is as follows:

    1. Formation of the Joint Venture; Identities of the Partners. We will form "Wirf den Ball, Gesmbh" (the JV") under the laws of Austria. The partners in the JV will be Southern California Kiddie Prints, Inc., a California

corporation ("Prints") and Leiser. The JV will operate under the name "Wirf den Ball" for all purposes. If and to the extent we are required in use an English name, the JV will operate under the name "Throw the Ball." The address of the JV will be at Leiser's current production facility.

2. <u>Purpose of the JV</u>. The purpose of the JV will be to manufacture and sell children's clothing, particularly pajamas, shirts, socks and shorts, all utilizing the Prints trademarked "Kiddie Prints" designs and names throughout the European Union.

3. <u>Duties and Obligations</u>. Prints will license to the JV all of its trademarked names and designs, free of charge to the JV, on an exclusive basis throughout the EU. We will mutually agree on the design of the clothing line that the JV will manufacture and sell. The production of the JV's products will be at Leiser's current production facility in Vienna on Leiser's equipment. Each partner will devote such time and efforts as may be necessary to design the product line and develop a sales force to market the JV's products. During the term of the JV, each partner will not sell any products in the EU that competes with the JV. Leiser will be free to sell other children's products in the EU for its own account, but will not sell any product that competes directly with any product being sold by the JV. Prints will be able to sell any product in the EU that does not compete with any product being sold by the JV.

4. <u>Capital Contributions</u>. Each partner shall be required to make the following initial capital contributions:

Leiser: € 100,000, plus all of those trademarks described in Exhibit A.

Prints: € 100,000, plus all of the machinery and equipment described in Exhibit B.

Neither of the partners will be required to contribute additional capital to the JV without the prior consent of the other. Once contributed, neither partner shall have the right to the return of its capital contribution except as by virtue of the distribution of JV profits.

5. <u>Management</u>. The JV will be managed by a Board of Directors ("Board") comprised of four persons. Each partner shall have the right to appoint two members to the Board. The unanimous consent of the Board shall be required to admit another partner to JV, assign an interest in the JV, or change the purpose of the JV. Each partner shall appoint a manager, who may also be a member of the Board. The unanimous consent of the managers shall be required in order to employ any employee, enter into any sales or purchasing contract, and set the sales prices of the JV's products.

6. <u>Allocations and Distributions Equally</u>. All gains, profits and increases that accrue from or by means of the JV business will be divided equally between the partners, and all losses that arise out of the business of the JV will be borne by and paid by the partners equally. No distributions shall be made to either partner without the consent of both managers.

7. <u>Term</u>. This Letter of Intent shall expire on June 30, 2014, or upon the earlier mutual consent of both parties. Upon the termination of this Letter of Intent, neither party hereto shall be under any obligation to each other with respect to this Letter of Intent or with respect to the transaction contemplated by this Letter of Intent.

All of the foregoing provisions of this Letter of Intent are non-binding. The following provisions are, however, intended to be legally binding upon both of the parties to this Letter of Intent, and shall remain binding upon them following the termination of the Term of this Letter of Intent:

1. <u>Confidentiality</u>. No party to this Letter of Intent shall disclose any Proprietary Information
to any third parties and will not use any Proprietary Information in that party's or any affiliated business without the prior written consent of the other party, and then only to the extent specified in the consent. Consent may be granted or withheld at the sole discretion of the other party. Neither party shall contact any suppliers, customers, employees or affiliates to circumvent the purposes of this section. Each party shall take all steps necessary or appropriate to maintain the strict the strict confidentiality of the proprietary information and to assure compliance with this Letter of Intent. For the purposes of this Letter of Intent, "Proprietary Information" shall include all information that would reasonably be considered proprietary or confidential to the business contemplated by this Letter of Intent, including but not limited to suppliers, marketing and technical plans, plans for products and ideas and proprietary techniques and other trade secrets.

2. <u>Non-Disclosure</u>. Neither party hereto shall disclose to any third person either the fact of this Letter of Intent, the joint venture contemplated by it, or any term contained herein, without the prior written consent of the other. Each party shall be permitted to disclose the existence and contents of this Letter of Intent only to those persons necessary in order to finalize a definitive agreement, including the parties' legal counsel, auditors, investment bankers and lenders.

If the above accurately summarizes our understanding of the formation and operating of joint venture, please execute the copy of this Letter of Intent where indicated below and return it to the undersigned. Immediately upon receipt of an executed copy, we will commence our mutual due diligence leading to the execution of a definitive and binding joint venture agreement.

Sincerely,

Southern California Kiddie Prints, Inc.
By:

_____

Its President

AGREED AND ACCEPTED:

Leiser Gmbh
By:

_____

Its President

EXHIBIT B

Joint Venture Agreement

THIS JOINT VENURE AGREEMENT, made and entered into as of this 1st day of March, 2014, by and between SOUTHERN CALIFORNIA KIDDIE PRINTS, INC., (herein, "SCKP") and LEISER Gmbh, (herein "Leiser"), is made pursuant to the following Recitals:

Recitals:

1. SCKP is engaged in the design, marketing and sale of trademarked children's apparel, including but not limited to children's pajamas, shirts, shorts and socks, all bearing the "Kiddie Prints™" trademarked designs, logotypes and styles throughout the United States of America.

2. Leiser is engaged in the manufacture and sale of apparel items throughout Austria and the European Union.

3. SCKP and Leiser desire to form a joint venture for the purpose of marketing children's apparel under the "Kiddie Prints" name and designs throughout the European Union, in accordance with the following terms and conditions.

NOW, THEREFORE, in consideration of the foregoing premises, and of the mutual representations, warranties, covenants and promises herein contained, the parties hereto stipulate and agree as follows:

1. <u>Formation of Joint Venture</u>. SCKP and Leiser hereby agree to form a joint venture under the law of Austria, which joint venture shall be known in Austria and throughout the European Union as "Wirf den Ball, GesmbH," and in the United States as "Throw the Ball." The joint venture will be incorporated under the laws of Austria. The address of the joint venture shall be at the corporate offices of Leiser, Boltzmanngasse 16, 1090 Vienna, Austria.

2. <u>Identities of the Partners</u>. The partners of the joint venture shall be Leiser, or an entity wholly-owned by Leiser whose sole function shall be to act as a joint venture partner, and "Kiddie Prints Austria GesmbH" a wholly-owned subsidiary of SCKP, whose sole function shall be to act as a joint venture partner. Unless specifically provided to the contrary herein, Leiser and SCKP, through their subsidiaries, shall be equal partners in every respect in the joint venture, with equal management rights, and equal rights in the allocation of profits, gains and distributions from the operations of the joint venture. Each of the partners shall receive a certificate representing 50% of the shares of Wirf den Ball, GesmbH, which shall be formed under the laws of Austria contemporaneously with the execution of this Joint Venture Agreement.

3. <u>Purpose of the Joint Venture</u>. The purpose of this joint venture shall be to design, manufacture, promote and sell for profit children's apparel, including pajamas, shirts, pants, socks, sheeting and baby blankets, throughout Austria and the European Union. All of the items of apparel manufactured by the joint venture shall bear the "Kiddie Prints" name and trademarks. The joint venture shall not engage in the sale of any items of apparel not contemplated by this Joint Venture Agreement, and shall not engage in the sale of any products outside of the

European Union or to any person intending the resale of any products produced by the joint venture outside of the European Union.

3.1 Activities Outside the Joint Venture.

        3.1.1 Nothing contained herein shall prevent SCKP from manufacturing, selling, licensing or otherwise dealing in the Kiddie Prints trademark and in the manufacture and sale of children's apparel anywhere in the world outside of the European Union. SCKP shall be prohibited from engaging in the sale of children's apparel in the European Union other than through the joint venture formed hereunder.

        3.1.2 Nothing contained herein shall prevent Leiser from manufacturing and selling items of apparel not bearing the Kiddie Prints trademarked logotype and design anywhere in the world.

    4. Duties and Obligations of the Partners. The parties hereto agree that SCKP shall be principally charged with the responsibility for the design of the items of apparel that the joint venture will sell throughout the European Union, and that Leiser shall be principally charged with the production of the items of apparel that the joint venture will market and sell throughout the European Union, at its current production facility at 16 Boltzmanngasse, Vienna. In addition, the parties hereto shall be equally responsible for the formulation and execution of sales and marketing plans.

    4.1 Duties and Obligations of SCKP. Contemporaneously with the execution of this Joint Venture Agreement, SCKP shall grant unto Wirf den Ball,

GesmbH, an exclusive license to produce, sell and otherwise deal in the "Kiddie Prints" registered trademarks, designs, logotypes and trade dress throughout the European Union, which license shall remain in full force and effect throughout the term of the Joint Venture, as defined hereinbelow. As long as the license is in effect, Wirf den Ball, GesmbH shall not be required to pay any royalty or other payment to SCKP in order to maintain its rights under the license.

4.1.1   SCKP shall have the principal duty, at its sole expense, to prosecute any person or entity whom SCKP reasonably believes to have infringed upon any trademark or other item of intellectual property licensed to the joint venture. In the event that SCKP is successful in obtaining a judgment, arbitrator's award or settlement (collectively "award") arising out of any claim instituted by SCKP on behalf of the joint venture, such award shall inure to the benefit of the joint venture, except that SCKP shall be entitled to first deduct its costs, including attorney's fees, in prosecuting any claimed infringement.

4.1.2   SCKP shall defend, at its sole expense, any claim that the licensed trademarks or other intellectual property assigned to the joint venture is invalid or infringes upon the intellectual property of any other party.

4.2 Duties and Obligations of Leiser. Leiser shall manufacture the items of apparel agreed upon by the parties hereto at its present production facility using the machinery and equipment that Leiser currently uses to manufacture apparel. If and to the extent Leiser is required to replace any items of machinery or equipment necessary to maintain production, Leiser shall do so, the cost of which shall be borne by the joint venture. Any replacement machinery and equipment shall be owned by the joint venture. Leiser shall not be entitled to receive any credit or offset for any wear and tear or depreciation to its current machinery and equipment used in the manufacture of the joint venture's apparel. Leiser shall be entitled to receive a credit for Leiser's cost of any existing items of inventory currently on hand and used by Leiser in the manufacture of any items of apparel at the commencement of the joint venture. Leiser shall assign those production managers, employees and others reasonably necessary to the business of the joint venture.

4.3 Mutual Duties and Obligations of Leiser and SCKP. As soon as practicable following the execution of this Joint Venture Agreement, Leiser and SCKP shall undertake to do the following:

4.3.1 formulate a plan for the design and production of a line of children's apparel bearing the "Kiddie Prints" trademarked name and logo.

4.3.2 formulate a plan for the advertising, promotion and marketing of the joint venture's trademarked apparel, including the engagement of a sales force and marketing managers, engaging advertising agencies public relations firms and representatives to deal with clothing wholesalers and retailers.

5. Initial Capital Contributions; Additional Capital Contributions. Leiser and SCKP, through their subsidiaries, if any, shall, in addition to the contributions to the joint venture described in Section 4, above, be required to contribute the cash sum of €100,000 to the joint venture. The initial capital contributions shall be expended towards the formation of Wirf den Ball, GesmbH, purchase of

machinery and equipment as the parties hereto shall agree to, engagement of a sales force and marketing personnel. Neither party hereto shall be entitled to the return of its initial capital contribution.

5.1 <u>Additional Capital Contributions</u>. It is the mutual intention of the parties hereto that increases in production or sales activities shall be funded solely out of the profits of the joint venture. Neither party shall be required to make any additional capital contributions to the joint venture, and all additional capital contributions shall be upon the consent of both partners.

6. <u>Management of the Joint Venture</u>. The joint venture shall be managed by a Board of Managing Directors, which shall be comprised of four Managing Directors, two of whom shall be nominated by each of the parties hereto or their subsidiaries. Each of the parties hereto, acting through their subsidiaries, shall vote to approve the nominees nominated by the other. The Managing Directors shall elect a Chairman of the Board of Managing Directors. In the event of a vacancy, the joint venture partner who shall have nominated the vacating Managing Director shall nominate a replacement Managing Director, and the other joint venture partner shall vote to approve such replacement.

6.1 <u>Duties of the Managing Directors</u>. The responsibility for the management of the joint venture shall rest in the Board of Managing Directors ("Board") acting as a body. The affirmative consent of a majority of the Board shall be required to take any action contemplated by this Joint Venture Agreement. The responsibilities of the Board shall include, but shall not be limited to, the following:

6.1.1 Directing all aspects of the design, manufacture, marketing and sale of the joint venture's products, including setting prices, purchasing inventory and equipment, engaging sales managers and other independent contractors.

6.1.2 Hiring a president and other executive officers, and determining the compensation and terms of employment of the president.

6.1.3 Engaging auditors, tax preparers, legal counsel and other professionals.

6.1.4 Determining the amount and timing of distributions of profits and excess cash to the partners, which in all events shall be distributed equally.

6.1.5 Borrowing funds and pledging joint venture assets as security therefore, maintaining banking relationships, entering into premises and other leases.

6.1.6 Establishing books of account, establishing a fiscal year for the joint venture, preparing and filing tax returns, payment of taxes and preparing accountings of profits and losses for the joint venture partners.

6.1.7 Instituting and defending claims and litigation.

6.2 Duties Reserved to SCKP. SCKP shall serve as the "Tax Matters Partner" for United States income tax purposes. SCKP shall have the sole responsibility to make any tax election with the taxing authorities of Austria, the United States or any other country in which the joint venture conducts business that might affect the United States federal income taxation of SCKP or its subsidiary, or SCKP's tax liability in any other jurisdiction.

6.3 <u>Duties Reserved to the President</u>. The president of the joint venture shall have the following duties, which the president shall undertake in his sole discretion, without the prior consent of the Board:

6.3.1 Controlling the production of the joint venture products.

6.3.2 Acquiring and disposing of items of inventory, machinery and equipment.

6.3.3 Granting rebates, concessions, and discounts of the joint venture's products.

6.3.4 Engaging and terminating non-executive employees, and setting the compensation and terms of employment of such employees.

6.4 <u>Actions Prohibited to the Board and the President</u>. Neither the Board, nor any member thereof, nor the President nor any other executive or non-executive officer shall engage in any conduct that would violate the United States Foreign Corrupt Practices Act ("FCPA") or any equivalent statute or rule of any other country. In the event that any member of the Board or any executive officer of the joint venture shall become aware of any claimed violation of the FCPA or any equivalent statute or rule, such person shall forthwith notify the Board of such claimed violation.

7.   Representations and Warranties of SCKP. SCKP represents and warrants unto Leiser and any subsidiary formed by Leiser to act as the joint venture partner, which representations and warranties shall survive the end of the Term of the joint venture, as follows:

7.1   Corporate Formation; Valid Existence. SCKP is a California corporation, duly formed and validly existing under the laws of California and in all of the jurisdictions in which it conducts its business. Nothing contained herein, and nothing contemplated by this Joint Venture Agreement may cause the breach of any agreement or undertaking to which SCKP is a party, or cause the acceleration of any indebtedness, or, to the best of SCKP's knowledge, result in the violation of any law, statute, ordinance, rule or regulation.

7.2   Consent to Enter into the Agreement. The Board of Directors of SCKP has approved this Joint Venture Agreement. The person executing this Joint Venture Agreement on behalf of SCKP has been duly authorized by SCKP's Board of Directors to enter into this Joint Venture Agreement and bind SCKP thereby.

7.3   Title to Assets. SCKP is the sole and rightful owner of all of the trademarks and other intellectual property being licensed hereby to Leiser. SCKP is not aware of any actual or threatened claim that SCKP's intellectual property violates the rights of any other person. SCKP has not instigated and does not contemplate instigating any claim or proceeding alleging that any other person has infringed upon any trademark or intellectual property right being licensed to Leiser hereunder.

7.4   Compliance with Laws. To the best of SCKP's knowledge, SCKP is not in breach of any law, statute, regulation, court order or ordinance of any kind, including but not limited to the United States Foreign Corrupt Practices Act, the violation of which would have a material effect upon the ability of SCKP to own its assets, conduct its business or carry out the duties and responsibilities contemplated by this Agreement.

8. <u>Representations and Warranties of Leiser</u>. Leiser represents and warrants unto SCKP and any subsidiary formed by Leiser to act as the joint venture partner, which representations and warranties shall survive the end of the Term of the joint venture, as follows:

8.1 <u>Corporate Formation; Valid Existence</u>. Leiser is an Austrian GesmbH, duly formed and validly existing under the laws of Austria and in all of the jurisdictions in which it conducts its business. Nothing contained herein, and nothing contemplated by this Joint Venture Agreement may cause the breach of any agreement or undertaking to which Leiser is a party, or cause the acceleration of any indebtedness, or, to the best of Leiser's knowledge, result in the violation of any law, statute, ordinance, rule or regulation.

8.2 <u>Consent to Enter into the Agreement</u>. The Board of Directors of Leiser has approved this Joint Venture Agreement. The person executing this Joint Venture Agreement on behalf of Leiser has been duly authorized by Leiser's Board of Directors to enter into this Joint Venture Agreement and bind Leiser thereby.

8.3 <u>Compliance with Laws</u>. To the best of Leiser's knowledge, Leiser is not in breach of any law, statute, regulation, court order or ordinance of any kind, including but not limited to Section 304, 305 and 306 of the Strafgesetzbuch, the violation of which would have a material effect upon the ability of Leiser to own its assets, conduct its business or carry out the duties and responsibilities contemplated by this Agreement.

9. <u>Restrictions on Transfer</u>. The parties hereto mutually agree that the efforts of each party hereby are unique, and that neither party would have entered into this Joint Venture Agreement with any other party. Accordingly, neither party hereto shall transfer its shares in Wirf den Ball, GesmbH, or its rights in and to this Joint Venture Agreement, to any person or entity, without the prior consent of the other party hereto, which consent may be withheld for any reason or for no reason. Any purported sale, exchange, assignment, encumbrance or other transfer, whether voluntarily, involuntarily or by operation of law, shall be null and void, and shall give any purported transferee no rights in and to this joint venture, or any of the rights, profits or distributions arising out of this Joint Venture.

10. <u>Term</u>. This joint venture shall commence upon the execution of this Joint Venture Agreement and the formation of Wirf den Ball, GesmbH, and shall continue until dissolved by the mutual consent of the parties or terminated as provided for herein below:

10.1 This joint venture shall terminate forthwith in the event that a neutral arbitrator appointed by the International Centre for Dispute Resolution shall have determined that a party hereto shall have violated a material breach of this Agreement, shall have breached its duty of fair dealing to the other party hereto, or shall have violated the United States Foreign Corrupt Practices Act, Sections 304, 305 or 306 of the Strafgesetzbuch of Austria or the equivalent statute or rule of any other country in which the joint venture conducts its business.

10.2 This joint venture shall terminate in the event that either party hereto files a petition seeking its reorganization in bankruptcy or files any similar petition in any court seeking its protection from creditors.

10.3 In the event that the Term of this joint venture is terminated for any reason, then:

10.3.1 The license of the trademarks, logotypes and other intellectual property previously granted to the joint venture by SCKP shall forthwith terminate, and all of the rights thereto shall revert to SCKP, without any further action on the part of SCKP.

10.3.2 The ownership of any machinery and equipment used by the joint venture shall be the sole and separate property of Leiser.

10.3.3 All of the cash, accounts receivable and other assets of the joint venture shall divided and distributed equally to the joint venture partners.

11. Dispute Resolution. In the event of any controversy or claim arising out of or relating to this agreement, or a breach thereof, the parties hereto agree first to try to settle the dispute by mediation, administered by the International Centre for Dispute Resolution under its Mediation Rules. If settlement is not reached within 60 days after service of a written demand for mediation, any unresolved controversy or claim arising out of or relating to this agreement shall be settled by arbitration in accordance with the International Arbitration Rules of the International Centre for Dispute Resolution."

DONE AND DATED as of the ___ day of March, 2014.

"SCKP"

Southern California Kiddie Prints, Inc.
By:

_____
President

"Leiser"

LEISER Gmbh
By:

_____
President

EXHIBIT C

Form **8832**	**Entity Classification Election**	
(Rev. December 2013)		OMB No. 1545-1516
Department of the Treasury Internal Revenue Service	▶ Information about Form 8832 and its instructions is at *www.irs.gov/form8832*.	

	Name of eligible entity making election	Employer identification number
Type or Print	Number, street, and room or suite no. If a P.O. box, see instructions.	
	City or town, state, and ZIP code. If a foreign address, enter city, province or state, postal code and country. Follow the country's practice for entering the postal code.	

▶ Check if: ☐ Address change ☐ Late classification relief sought under Revenue Procedure 2009-41
☐ Relief for a late change of entity classification election sought under Revenue Procedure 2010-32

Part I **Election Information**

1 **Type of election** (see instructions):

a ☐ Initial classification by a newly-formed entity. Skip lines 2a and 2b and go to line 3.
b ☐ Change in current classification. Go to line 2a.

2a Has the eligible entity previously filed an entity election that had an effective date within the last 60 months?

☐ **Yes.** Go to line 2b.
☐ **No.** Skip line 2b and go to line 3.

2b Was the eligible entity's prior election an initial classification election by a newly formed entity that was effective on the date of formation?

☐ **Yes.** Go to line 3.
☐ **No.** Stop here. You generally are not currently eligible to make the election (see instructions).

3 Does the eligible entity have more than one owner?

☐ **Yes.** You can elect to be classified as a partnership or an association taxable as a corporation. Skip line 4 and go to line 5.
☐ **No.** You can elect to be classified as an association taxable as a corporation or to be disregarded as a separate entity. Go to line 4.

4 If the eligible entity has only one owner, provide the following information:

a Name of owner ▶
b Identifying number of owner ▶

5 If the eligible entity is owned by one or more affiliated corporations that file a consolidated return, provide the name and employer identification number of the parent corporation:

a Name of parent corporation ▶
b Employer identification number ▶

For Paperwork Reduction Act Notice, see instructions.   Cat. No. 22598R   Form **8832** (Rev. 12-2013)

Form 8832 (Rev. 12-2013)   Page **2**

Part I   **Election Information** (Continued)

6   **Type of entity** (see instructions):

a ☐ A domestic eligible entity electing to be classified as an association taxable as a corporation.

b ☐ A domestic eligible entity electing to be classified as a partnership.

c ☐ A domestic eligible entity with a single owner electing to be disregarded as a separate entity.

d ☐ A foreign eligible entity electing to be classified as an association taxable as a corporation.

e ☐ A foreign eligible entity electing to be classified as a partnership.

f ☐ A foreign eligible entity with a single owner electing to be disregarded as a separate entity.

7   If the eligible entity is created or organized in a foreign jurisdiction, provide the foreign country of organization ▶

8   Election is to be effective beginning (month, day, year) (see instructions) . . . . ▶

9   Name and title of contact person whom the IRS may call for more information   **10** Contact person's telephone number

Consent Statement and Signature(s) (see instructions)

Under penalties of perjury, I (we) declare that I (we) consent to the election of the above-named entity to be classified as indicated above, and that I (we) have examined this election and consent statement, and to the best of my (our) knowledge and belief, this election and consent statement are true, correct, and complete. If I am an officer, manager, or member signing for the entity, I further declare under penalties of perjury that I am authorized to make the election on its behalf.

Signature(s)	Date	Title

Form **8832** (Rev. 12-2013)

EXHIBIT D

Form 8865

Department of the Treasury
Internal Revenue Service

Return of U.S. Persons With Respect to Certain Foreign Partnerships

▶ Attach to your tax return.
▶ Information about Form 8865 and its separate instructions is at *www.irs.gov/form8865*.
Information furnished for the foreign partnership's tax year
beginning _____, 2013, and ending _____, 20___

OMB No. 1545-1668

2013

Attachment
Sequence No. **118**

Name of person filing this return

Filer's identifying number

Filer's address (if you are not filing this form with your tax return)

A Category of filer (see **Categories of Filers** in the instructions and check applicable box(es))
1 ☐ 2 ☐ 3 ☐ 4 ☐

B Filer's tax year beginning _____, 20___ and ending _____, 20___

C Filer's share of liabilities: Nonrecourse $ _____ Qualified nonrecourse financing $ _____ Other $ _____

D If filer is a member of a consolidated group but not the parent, enter the following information about the parent:
Name _____ EIN _____
Address _____

E Information about certain other partners (see instructions)

(1) Name	(2) Address	(3) Identifying number	(4) Check applicable box(es)		
			Category 1	Category 2	Constructive owner

F1 Name and address of foreign partnership

2(a) EIN (if any)

2(b) Reference ID number (see instr.)

3 Country under whose laws organized

4 Date of organization	5 Principal place of business	6 Principal business activity code number	7 Principal business activity	8a Functional currency	8b Exchange rate (see instr.)

G Provide the following information for the foreign partnership's tax year:

1 Name, address, and identifying number of agent (if any) in the United States

2 Check if the foreign partnership must file:
☐ Form 1042 ☐ Form 8804 ☐ Form 1065 or 1065-B
Service Center where Form 1065 or 1065-B is filed.

3 Name and address of foreign partnership's agent in country of organization, if any

4 Name and address of person(s) with custody of the books and records of the foreign partnership, and the location of such books and records, if different

5 Were any special allocations made by the foreign partnership? .... ▶ ☐ Yes ☐ No

6 Enter the number of Forms 8858, Information Return of U.S. Persons With Respect To Foreign Disregarded Entities, attached to this return (see instructions) .... ▶ _____

7 How is this partnership classified under the law of the country in which it is organized? ▶ _____

8a Does the filer have an interest in the foreign partnership, or an interest indirectly through the foreign partnership, that is a separate unit under Reg. 1.1503(d)-1(b)(4) or part of a combined separate unit under Reg. 1.1503(d)-1(b)(4)(ii)? If "No," skip question 8b. ▶ ☐ Yes ☐ No

b If "Yes," does the separate unit or combined separate unit have a dual consolidated loss as defined in Reg. 1.1503(d)-1(b)(5)(ii)? ▶ ☐ Yes ☐ No

9 Does this partnership meet **both** of the following requirements?
• The partnership's total receipts for the tax year were less than $250,000 and
• The value of the partnership's total assets at the end of the tax year was less than $1 million.
If "Yes," **do not** complete Schedules L, M-1, and M-2. .... ▶ ☐ Yes ☐ No

Sign Here Only If You Are Filing This Form Separately and Not With Your Tax Return.

Under penalties of perjury, I declare that I have examined this return, including accompanying schedules and statements, and to the best of my knowledge and belief, it is true, correct, and complete. Declaration of preparer (other than general partner or limited liability company member) is based on all information of which preparer has any knowledge.

▶ Signature of general partner or limited liability company member ▶ Date

Paid Preparer Use Only

Print/Type preparer's name	Preparer's signature	Date	Check ☐ if self-employed	PTIN
Firm's name ▶			Firm's EIN ▶	
Firm's address ▶			Phone no.	

For Privacy Act and Paperwork Reduction Act Notice, see the separate instructions. Cat. No. 25852A Form **8865** (2013)

About the Authors

Robert Klueger J.D., LL.M

Robert F. Klueger received his B.A. from the University of Pennsylvania (cum laude), his law degree from Fordham Law School, and his Master of Laws in Taxation from the University of Denver. He has been accredited by the State Bar of California as a Certified Tax Law Specialist, is AV-rated (highest possible rating) by Martindale-Hubbell and has been named "A Super Lawyer" by the Los Angeles Magazine.

A practicing attorney since 1974, he is a member of the bars of the United States Supreme Court, the United States Tax Court and the state bars of California, New York and Colorado.

He is one of the very few private attorneys in America who has argued a tax case before the United States Supreme Court, [United States v. Brockamp, 519 U.S. 347 (1997)], which resulted in a change in the tax law regarding tax refund claims filed by disabled taxpayers.

Mr. Klueger is a frequent lecturer on structuring business transactions, choice of entity and sophisticated tax planning. He has lectured extensively throughout the United States. He is the author of numerous books and scholarly articles.

About the Authors

Jacob Stein, J.D., LL.M

Mr. Stein received his law degree from the University of Southern California, and his Master of Law in Taxation from Georgetown University. He has been accredited by the State Bar of California as a Certified Tax Law Specialist, is AV-rated (highest possible rating) by Martindale-Hubbell and has been named "A Super Lawyer" by the Los Angeles Magazine.

Over the course of his career Mr. Stein has represented officers and directors of Fortune 500 companies; Forbes 400 families; celebrities; Internet entrepreneurs; Nobel prize laureates; businesses of all sizes engaging in cross-border transactions; and wealthy foreigners doing business in the United States.

Mr. Stein is an author of numerous books, scholarly articles and technical manuals and is a frequent lecturer, teaching over 50 seminars per year. He is an adjunct professor of taxation at the CSU, Northridge Graduate Tax Program.

INDEX

NOTES

www.ingramcontent.com/pod-product-compliance
Lightning Source LLC
Chambersburg PA
CBHW070409200326

41518CB000118/2126